Go!
Navigate Your Way To Success

Napoleon Hill
&
George Harrison Phelps

PRABHAT
PRAKASHAN

Published by
PRABHAT PRAKASHAN PVT. LTD.
4/19 Asaf Ali Road,
New Delhi-110 002 (INDIA)
e-mail: prabhatbooks@gmail.com

Published in India by arrangement with
The Napoleon Hill Foundation
PO Box 1277, Wise, Virginia 24293, USA

ISBN 978-93-5186-777-7
GO! Navigate Your Way to Success
by Napoleon Hill & George Harrison Phelps

Edition
2026

Paperback Price
₹ 450.00 (Rupees Four Hundred Fifty only)

Printed at
Shree Sai Printers, Sahibabad

Contents

Foreword

by Judith Williamson

Dear Readers,

Go! Navigate Your Way to Success is a book filled with stories that entertain and teach simultaneously. There are 51 short tales that are matched item per item to a lesson that Dr. Napoleon Hill himself has written. Also, placed throughout the pages are contemporary commentaries by individuals who value and use Dr. Hill's success teachings. Each essay is dedicated to telling a story and then making a point. Not only will you enjoy the story, but you will also gain a valuable success lesson that stays in your memory bank. And, at just the right moment when you need the teaching, you will recall the story and apply the lesson to your benefit.

The selections from Dr. Hill's teachings are taken from his earliest works that include *Napoleon Hill's Magazine, The Law of Success, Think and Grow Rich,* and one excerpt from *How to Attract Men and Money.* I feel that these selections fit best within the historical context of the stories used to illustrate the lessons. It is interesting to note that success stories of this nature are available in all walks of life, but in order to extract the lesson and put it to personal use, the reader must ask three questions: First, "What is the lesson or moral of the story?" Next, "How does the lesson correspond to or enhance the story?" And, finally, "How does this apply to me right now, today?"

Stories on salesmanship, self-discipline, personal initiative, going the extra mile, tolerance, pleasing personality, applied faith, learning from adversity and defeat and many more topics are all included in the 51 brief but thought provoking stories. Like little vignettes on life, each story captures a glimpse into a person's success consciousness. When we train ourselves to look at someone else's patterns of behavior, it then encourages us to critique our own patterns that either work for or against us.

If life is a journey, it only makes sense to believe that having a guiding compass to assist us in our daily navigation would make things easier. By knowing whether we are traveling in the proper direction or moving toward our ultimate destination, we can better calculate our outcome. Pretending that our life's compass has Dr. Hill's 17 Principles of Success on its faceplate will help us pinpoint principles that we need to traverse if we are going to reach our definite major purpose. Seeing the journey of life in this fashion allows us to believe that we do have control over the itinerary and ultimate destination we choose for ourselves. Although each of our journeys is unique because it is ours alone, it also mirrors the journeys taken by others throughout time. Comparing and contrasting our similarities and differences with others permits us to analyze how we can better make our trip a more comfortable, enjoyable, and advantageous one for ourselves. We do know that the map is not the actual terrain we will trek. However, by having a map and guiding compass we can anticipate the ups and downs of the road ahead in order to better prepare ourselves for the adventure.

Now, with knapsack, tent, and compass in hand, go forth and enjoy the journey.

Be Your Very Best Always,
Judy Williamson

At the Galley's Oar

George Harrison Phelps

You are in the Roman Coliseum. It is the afternoon of the great chariot race. The amphitheatre is packed with people. The women are gorgeously arrayed in blue and crimson and gold. Patricians, poets, statesmen, philosophers, warriors—many in brilliant costumes—lend life and gayety to the shifting scene. The gigantic bowl is alive with light and color. The air is tense with excitement.

The great race of the day is almost ended. The charioteers are nearing the last turn to finish in front of the royal stand. Everyone leans forward. There is no sound throughout the vast Coliseum save the rush of the flying horses, the thunder of the chariots, the cries of the charioteers.

The speed is terrific. Ben Hur is driving in second place. They approach the last corner. The leaders pitch forward. Driver and chariot and horses all roll in front of Ben Hur.

Like a flash he takes a double hold on the reins and, fairly lifting the horses, drives them over the prostrate bodies in his path.

As he swings into the stretch, Artimidora cries to him from the royal box: "Those arms—where did you get those arms?" He shouts in answer: *"At the Galley's Oar! At the Galley's Oar!"*

In the hold of a trireme, Ben Hur got those mighty arms that carried him to victory. For years he slaved at a great oar among the hundred other slaves—half naked and sweating—the lash at his back.

"Do the thing and you shall have the power," said Emerson. After Ben Hur's years of Herculean toil it was an easy task to lift the horses over the wrecked chariot and drive them to the front.

All great things are accomplished easily—it is the years, the hours, the moments of preparation that count. Thomas Edison was not twenty minutes proving the value of the incandescent light—he spent half a lifetime seeking the best filament. Abraham Lincoln wrote the greatest speech ever made in the English language—the Gettysburg Address—on the back of an envelope, an hour before he delivered it—yet, the deep understanding, the rugged spirit, the infinite compassion, the whole life of Lincoln thrills in its every word.

Work, constantly, patiently, every day—striving toward the highest and the best. The moments of supreme action will come to you as they have come to all men we call great. The way of success is the way of struggle. Strive for perfection in the little things you do, and when the great moment comes you will be ready. You get your strength in the sweat of your body—in the tumult of your mind—in the aspiration of your soul.

To win the race you must first be a slave at the galley's oar.

Achievement is Born of Sacrifice

Napoleon Hill

There can be no great achievement without a corresponding sacrifice. Christ gave his life that his philosophy might be planted in the human heart forever.

Think of one person, if you can, who has risen to fame or rendered the world a lasting service without sacrifice. Usually the value of the service rendered is in proportion to the sacrifice out of which it sprung.

Nature does not appear to favor the perpetuation of ideas or ideals which are not born of sacrifice and nurtured amid hardship and struggle. From the lowest mineral substance to the highest form of animal organism nature gives evidence aplenty of Her favoritism for that which is born of hardship, resistance and struggle.

The hardiest and finest trees of the forest are those which grew slowly and overcame the greatest resistance. No hot-house vegetable can equal those that are grown in the open, in opposition to the elements of the weather.

In a practical, material world of business, finance and industry we see evidence on every hand of the soundness of this philosophy. Successes that are achieved overnight seldom endure. The greatest achievements in business are those which began at the very bottom, were based upon sound fundamentals and experienced seemingly impossible sacrifice. Before we envy Henry Ford his success we should meditate upon the struggles and hardships which he survived before he created the first Ford automobile. All of us would enjoy his great wealth but few of us would be willing to pay for it in sacrifice, as he has done.

If you are taking your baptism of fire and paying the price of sacrifice with faith in your handiwork, no matter what station in life you are striving to achieve you are apt to realize it if you carry on without losing faith, without turning back, without losing confidence in yourself and in the fundamental principle which insures achievement that corresponds to the nature and extent of your sacrifice.

Source: *Napoleon Hill's Magazine*. February, 1922, inside back cover.

Mike McDonald

George Harrison Phelps

If you know it's true—if you know you're right—don't be afraid to say, "By God, this way it is!" Never mind the sneers and jibes. Make your own chart and hold your course. Right will always go ahead, and prove itself at last. Forget Custom and Tradition, for they are only barnacles on your ship of Success. They fix the limits of progress for the man who never dares to break the bonds.

One night I sat chinning with the Big Boss and he told me the story of Old Mike McDonald. Perhaps you will find a bit of inspiration in it—anyway, here it is:

Old McDonald was editor of a Western paper, one of that great race of pioneer literary supermen now fast disappearing from the earth. Mike was of the species that is kindly yet gruffly stern, and his word was another term for law.

One of his chief diversions was to make big blue rings around words his "cub" reporters wrote. Mike was a "bug" on spelling. Often he would lean over a reporter's shoulder and correct copy that was just begun. Some of the "cubs," who deemed it their special duty to keep Noah Webster's grave strewn with fresh flowers, occasionally uttered great and joyous shouts of triumph when, on consulting the big and tattered dictionary in the office corner, they found that Webster stood with them and not with Mike McDonald. Then, if courageous enough, they told Mike about it.

But, strangely, such a discovery never made much difference with Mike. The word went into the paper as he had corrected it. Even the "bible of Webster" couldn't shake him. He felt that he was right—and he stuck.

On such occasions the "cubs" sniffed the air and smiled scornful smiles behind his back. "Bullhead," they muttered. And they repeated it with added emphasis on discovering that Mike had not only ordered his version run in the paper but had put the same blue mark on Old Noah himself. He had corrected the dictionary!

One day Mike laid down his big blue pencil for the last time and crossed the river to where spelling doesn't matter much. His dictionary was kicked about the office for months. Nobody noticed it now. Finally it came to the attention of a new man on the staff—a man who recognized and appreciated courageous originality. He packed Mike's book in a box and sent it to the publisher.

The next edition of the dictionary contained most of Mike's corrections.

Have you the nerve to be a Mike McDonald?

Self-Confidence

Napoleon Hill

> *Our doubts are traitors, and make us lose the good we oft might win by fearing to attempt. – Shakespeare*

Lincoln started in a log hut and stopped in the White House—because he believed in himself. Napoleon began as a poor Corsican and brought half of Europe to his feet— because he believed in himself. Henry Ford started as a poor farmer lad and put more wheels into motion than any other man on earth—because he believed in himself. Rockefeller started as a poor bookkeeper and became the world's richest man—because he believed in himself. They took that which they wished because they had confidence in their own ability. Now, the question is, WHY DO YOU NOT DECIDE WHAT YOU WANT, THEN GO OUT AND TAKE IT?

Source: *Napoleon Hill's Magazine.* April, 1923, p. 2.

Harriman

George Harrison Phelps

Emerson has said that an institution is but the lengthened shadow of a man. It is that—and more. It is a man. Somewhere in every organization, big or little, you will find one dominating personality, a subtle force that controls the destinies of the business. Look around you in any crowd or company and you will see one person whose personality charges the very atmosphere; one man, or one woman, who quietly and almost imperceptibly draws the attention of all the others.

Why? Ask the steel why it clings to the magnet.

Personality, like electricity, is indefinable.

It is recognized only by its manifestations.

The physical appearance of its conductor matters very little.

It is said that Napoleon's presence before his troops would instantly change them from the depths of despair to a stage of wildest enthusiasm. Sankey, the blind evangelist singer, has been known to quiet a mob of strikers with a few bars from a familiar hymn.

E. H. Harriman, that wonderful genius of transportation, was not a prepossessing man in appearance. He was small in stature, and during the period of his greatest power he was almost constantly ill. And yet he moulded the surface of America as he willed, that he might knit the nation's railway resources together for the common good.

John Muir, the sage of the Sierras, says: "He seemed to regard the whole continent as his farm and all the people as his pastures, steering by his personality millions of workers into useful action, plowing, sowing, irrigating, mining, building cities and factories, farms and homes."

Once in a conference with Otto Kahn, the great banker, he asked Mr. Kahn to assist him in securing an appointment to the directorate of a certain road. "I don't really see what use this would be to you," said Mr. Kahn. "You would be one of fifteen men of whom presumable fourteen would be against you." Mr. Harriman replied: "I know that, but all the opportunity I ever want is to be one of fifteen men around a table."

His life-work shows that he spoke the truth. Through sickness and sorrow and physical handicap his personality carried him on—that force that makes one man different from another—one man strong and another weak. It is the chief asset of a successful man. It distinguishes you from the human tide that ebbs and flows across the sands of business.

Cultivate it. Make yourself predominate.

Foretell Your Own Future

Napoleon Hill

If you are interested in your own future practically any man of intelligence can help you read it quite accurately if you will answer these questions:

First: Do you practice the habit of doing more work than you are paid for?

Second: Do you depend upon your own plans and your own efforts for advancement?

Third: Have you trained yourself to do the thing that ought to be done without someone telling you to do it?

Fourth: Do you understand the principle of CAUSE and EFFECT?

Fifth: Do you wait for opportunities to show up, or quietly go about creating them?

Answer these five questions correctly and even the most elementary thinker can foretell what your finish will be.

You are living in the most advantageous age in the entire history of the world, and regardless of what your present station in life may be or how humble your beginning, the possibilities ahead of you stagger the imagination. You are living in an age that affords every needed stimulant to arouse your imagination and inspire you with ambition.

Source: *Napoleon Hill's Magazine*. May–June, 1923, p. 36.

Path to Greatness

Phil Barlow

Greatness is not a function of circumstance. It is a result of conscious choice and discipline by people who have a burning desire to achieve greatness. Take a look at any organization that has achieved extraordinary performance and you will find people whose personalities infect the entire organization with enthusiasm and confidence. The attributes of their personalities are contagious and attach like a magnet to others in the organization.

The power of choice is a remarkable thing. It is one of the greatest powers bestowed on the human race. A pleasing personality is not something we're born with. It's something we can choose to develop throughout our lives. It's encouraging to know the traits of a pleasing personality are within the reach of the humblest person. Regardless of age, physical stature, race, social environment or habitat, you can choose to develop a pleasing personality. It all starts with taking a personal inventory of who you are and then committing to change bad habits into good ones and improving on the good habits you have.

Every time you come in contact with another person or groups of people, you leave them with an impression. How do they really feel about the experience? Do they feel better or worse as a result of it? Does your personality have anything to do with how they feel?

Absolutely!

Your personality is your greatest asset or liability. It can attract other people to you like a magnet or repel them like a bad odor. It embraces everything you control through the power of choice: your mind, body and soul. Personality is the most important factor that determines whether a person is liked or disliked by others. Having effective relationships and interaction with others, to a large degree, will determine the success of any individual.

It's important to always be considerate of others. Being genuinely interested in other people and respecting their dignity is one sure way to develop a pleasing personality, the personality that attracts like a magnet. Above all, observe the golden rule; treat others as you would like to be treated. If you treat others the way you would like to be treated, you will not have to worry about whether people like you or not.

You personality is entirely up to you. You have the power of choice right at your fingertips. You can choose to have a pleasing personality or you can choose not to. What is your choice?

At the Dardanelles

George Harrison Phelps

The difference between success and failure is frequently only a matter of persistency. Just a little more courage, a little more patience, and the prospective customer you gave up yesterday as impregnable might be turned into an order today.

Of course you have heard the secret of the siege of Gallipoli. You know how the Allies hammered away with great guns for weeks and months at the gates of the Dardanelles. Success at that point might have meant success all through the war. The Allies knew it—the Turks and Germans knew it.

Both battled desperately. Food supplies within the gates began to dwindle. Ammunition ran low. Then came the hour of the crisis.

Sixty minutes more and the last shell would have been spent in the cause of defense. Sixty minutes to go!

Then, suddenly, the sound of the British cannon died away. A message flashed in from an outpost on the shore. The fleet was moving away! The British had quit. They had given up the attack as futile.

In sixty minutes more the Turks would have been forced to surrender. The walls of Stamboul would have been crushed under the feet of the invader. The key of success would have been snatched from the Turkish hands.

Think of the order that British admiral lost! An order for the richest price of the war—the key to the Dardanelles.

Just a little more courage—a little more patience—a little more persistency. Sixty minutes more was all he needed. "He didn't know," you say, "that the Turk's ammunition was almost exhausted? He didn't know that the forts would have ceased belching fire in another hour? He didn't know that he could have marched into a soldier-less city at dawn?"

That's just it—he didn't know.

How many times has this happened to you? How many times have you found your prospect buying from a rival salesman when you might have won if you had stood by your guns?

Take a lesson from the Dardanelles.

Stay for the finish.

Don't quit.

Persistency

Napoleon Hill

Persistency and concentration are so closely related that it is hard to say where is the line which separates them.

Persistency is synonymous with will power or determination. It is the quality which causes you to keep the powers of your mind focused upon a given objective, through the principle of concentration, until that objective has been reached.

Persistence is the quality which causes you to arise, when once you have been knocked down by temporary failure, and continue your pursuit of a given desire or object. It is the quality which gives you courage and faith to keep on trying in the face of any and all obstacles which may confront you. It is the quality which causes the bulldog to find the death grip on his opponent's throat and then lie down and hold on in spite of all efforts to shake him off.

However, you are not aiming to develop persistency for the purpose of using it as the bulldog does. You are developing it for the purpose of carrying you over those necessary rocks and reefs which nearly every person must master in reaching any worth-while place in the world. You are developing persistency to guide you unwavering in a given direction only after you are satisfied that you are going in the right direction. Indiscriminate use of persistency might only get you in trouble.

Source: *Napoleon Hill's Magazine.* April, 1921, p. 36.

Let Them Laugh

George Harrison Phelps

Figure out a plan for the thing you want to do. Do it in spite of Hell! The creature who first said "Impossible" was a pigmy. He had a flunkey's soul. Nothing is impossible. All barriers fall when one has the nerve to fight. Napoleon's lieutenants protested that the Alps could not be crossed. He answered: "There shall be no Alps." The Spartans at Thermopylae were told that the Persian hordes could not be held at bay. The Spartans held the pass. "You cannot drive away the darkness with your filament of clay," cried Science. But Edison lit the world.

Forever the impossibilities of yesterday are hatching into facts today. "It can't be done" usually is interrupted by a newsboy shouting that it has been done. "Uxtry, uxtry—." A man reads the triumphant story of a *completed* something on which his *fancies* had dwelt for years. To him the newsboy's shout is the signal of a thing that *might have been*—had he but done it. But he had anchored his fate on hope, and the anchor line was of silk, and slender—it snapped. Each day lines are snapping. Each day the thing that you *might have* done is done by others.

Edison's greatness is not alone in his inventions. Had he faltered, others would have been there to take his place. The world would not have waited. Edison knew. He figured out his plan, and he won. Now we press the button and the night is day. Edison is great because he was the first to finish the job.

The twentieth century taste demanded a fruit that was new. It was the cue for Burbank. He stuck to his plan and worked it out. Our breakfast table today is laid with fruits our grandfathers never heard of.

America dug Panama. Others failed, but America mapped out a plan, steamed up its dredges on determination—and did it. The others had been dreamers, spurred on and checked alternately by visions of a canal completed and by collisions with obstacles unforeseen. They hadn't prepared to go through with their plan. There wasn't enough powder behind their push.

They laughed at Columbus when he said he could sail away from Asia and yet reach it. But Columbus did it, and he gave to the world New York, San Francisco, the North Pole and the Horn and all that lies between. Let them laugh if they will—then show them.

The salesman who can't occasionally turn a smile of derision into a gasp of admiration is wasting his time at the business. Tell them it *can* be done, then do it. Their laugh will not last and your courage will tighten. You *did* it—and you can do it again. Just figure out a plan of the thing you want.

Then *get* it.

Life's Trump Card!

Napoleon Hill

Laugh, and the world laughs with you;
Weep, and you weep alone.
For the sad old earth must borrow its mirth,
But has trouble enough of its own.
Sing, and the hills will answer;

Sign, it is lost on the air.
The echoes bound to a joyful sound,
But shrink from voicing care.

If you come with a joyful song on your lips the whole world will welcome and applaud you, but, if you come with a tale of woe you will find no listeners.

It will make a sight of difference to you whether you are a person with a message or a grievance. People will sometimes listen to a tale of woe, but they never cultivate the person who bears it. "I am too busy with my own troubles to be burdened with yours," says the world.

Nagging never reformed a wayward boy nor a night-owl husband, and it never will! Talk about men's virtues and you will get their undivided attention, but mention their faults and they will soon find business around the corner.

He is a wise man who finds out what people wish to hear and talks about it, but the reformer has a hard time holding his audience.

How strange that this psychological principle is not better understood and more often applied. If married women understood it there would be slim chance for "the other woman" to create the eternal triangle, and if parents applied the principle the back alley sports would be poor competitors for the fireside circle.

If you have troubles and must air them, do not speak them, but write them—write them in the sands, near the water's edge.

Many a man has sought companionship outside of his own home for no other reason that his dislike for the tales of woe his companion poured into his ears when he was around. The attractive personality is the one that speaks of the good there is in people, overlooks the bad and always gives more credit than is due, never less.

The most beautiful character on earth is the one that always brings along the old kit bag well filled with glad tidings, leaves all troubles at home, has at least one good word to say about the village loafer, and never forgets to smile when others frown. Oh to be such a person.

Rejoice, and men will seek you;
Grieve, and they turn and go.
They want full measure of all your pleasure,
But they do not need your woe.
Be glad, and your friends are many;
Be sad, and you lose them all.
There are none to decline your nectared wine,
But alone you must drink life's gall.

Source: *Napoleon Hill's Magazine.* October, 1921, p. 18.

Play Up and Play the Game

George Harrison Phelps

When I was in college there was a man at Princeton named Eddie Hart. He was a real man. When I think of him I think of Kipling's Fuzzy Wuzzy, in which he says, "You're a poor benighted heathen, but a damned good fighting man."

Of course, Hart was neither poor nor benighted. He was a stupendous success in college, and he has since risen high in the business world. He has made good under conditions that would give the ordinary man arteriosclerosis.

For three years he was captain of the Princeton football team, and every year he made brighter the name and fame of the Orange and Black. He was a born leader and he had the indomitable courage of a matador. During his third year, in a tough battle on a slushy field, he broke his neck and was carried out for dead. And he might have died then and there, or he might have lain flat on his back in a hospital for the remainder of his life. But he didn't. His fine come-back was due partly to luck, but mostly, I think, as I remember him, to his "damned good fighting spirit."

After lying still for a few weeks he had a special harness made to hold his head from resting on his spine, and with this strapped to his great shoulders he startled the world by appearing again at the head of his team.

He used to carry around in his pocket the school song of Eton. He said it was the spirit of this song that made him win.

I believe it—and I believe that it holds a message for the man who would win at anything. Here's a part of it:

The sand of the river is sodden red,
Red with the wreck of a square that broke;
The gatling's jammed and the colonel dead
And the regiment blind with dust and smoke.
The river of Death has brimmed its banks,
And England's far and Honor a name,
But the voice of a schoolboy rallies the ranks,
"Play up! Play up! and play the game!"

When I think of Hart playing against Harvard and Yale and winning with a broken neck—every moment in danger of snapping the slender cord of life—I haven't much patience with the salesman or dealer who has all his organs and faculties in perfect order and crying for action, and yet sits and bemoans the fact that he has had a cancellation or two—that the weather is hot—that he can't get enough cars to fill his orders.

It's *nerve* he needs—nerve to rustle out for two new sales for every one he's lost.

That's why I'm telling the story of Eddie Hart.

That's why I say:

"Buck up! Buck up! and play the game!"

Brace Up, Man!

Napoleon Hill

Brace up, Man! Up—and stop worrying. The game of life is never lost until you accept defeat. Trusted friends will fail you as they have failed others before your time. You will try and fail and try and fail again, as millions of others have done. Waste no time fretting about this. It is only a repetition of that which has been taking place all back down the ages. You can wear only one suit of clothes at a time and you can eat only one plate of ham and eggs at a sitting, and the things you worry about probably will never happen, and, if they did you would not know the difference a hundred years from now; therefore, sit down in some quiet spot and calm yourself while the thought soaks into your head that the best policy is to take life as it comes without permitting anything or anyone either to break your heart or overwhelm you with joy.

Source: *Napoleon Hill's Magazine.* March, 1922, back cover.

On the Job

George Harrison Phelps

I had known the man for several years. I had seen him climb to affluence and position and power in one of the greatest packing houses in the world. Steadily he had climbed, and slowly—never faltering. Then, one day he took a leap ahead that placed him at the very top of his business. As he departed from his birthland for London to assume control of the European business for his firm I marveled at the indefinable, invisible power that must be hidden in his big frame. Often I wondered what it was inside this great, good-natured man that drove him on so steadily.

One day I found out. Let me pass the story on to you.

On a morning shortly after war was declared the Chicago office of this packing house was humming with repressed excitement. Word had been received from an European power that only a guarantee of immediate delivery was necessary for an almost fabulous order for beef—millions, many millions, it counted. Quick action was necessary—someone must be at this nation's war office at once! A list of available transports must be had, and there was only one man who could handle the details that would win this gigantic contract. He was on his vacation, somewhere on the continent—no one knew exactly where.

At 10 o'clock in the morning a cable flashed from Chicago to London—"Where is Hall?" Definite advices must be in the hands of the minister of war before night. Representatives of other firms, equally well prepared, were already racing toward

Paris. It all meant millions. The hours dragged slowly for the officials in Chicago. They waited impatiently—all thought abandoned save the message from across the sea. They knew that its contents would mean the loss or gain of the greatest single order of its kind ever placed.

A few minutes past 3 o'clock—or just five hours after the inquiry had flashed to London, the answer came—a message that today is inscribed in the records of this firm as evidence of the highest type of salesmanship and initiative. It was brief—from the war office, Paris:

"I am on the job. Transports being loaded. Hall."

This man had closed the deal! He had heard that the French government must have beef and have it quickly. He stopped at nothing. Leaving his family in a little town near Luzerne, he rushed on to Paris, gathering information as he went—lists of transports that could be commandeered; all the ammunition necessary to win this great battle of salesmanship.

I marvel no longer at the man's success. Now I know the secret.

He was *on the job.*

Initiative

Napoleon Hill

Initiative is that very rare quality which impels a person to do that which ought to be done without *being told to do it!* All great leaders must possess initiative. A man without initiative could never become a great general, either in warfare or in business and industry, because generalship, to be successful, must be based on intense *action*.

Golden opportunities are lurking at every corner, waiting for the person with initiative to come along and discover them. When a person performs only the tasks allotted to him and then stops he attracts no particular attention, but, when he take the *initiative,* and goes ahead and looks for other tasks to be performed after his regular duties have been taken care of, *attracts the favorable attention of his superiors* who willingly allot to him greater responsibilities, with pay accordingly.

Before a person can rise high in any field of endeavor he must become a person of vision, who can think in big terms, who can create *definite* plans and then carry these plans into *action,* all of which make it imperative that the quality of initiative be developed.

Source: *Napoleon Hill's Magazine.* April, 1921, p. 32.

The Prophet

George Harrison Phelps

The winding trail along which the young man climbed was steep and narrow. The sharp stones cut his feet and frequently he stumbled to his knees—but always he continued his journey upward toward the top of the mountain. The battle he was fighting with himself had dulled his sense of pain. Each jagged rock seemed only to quicken his shame as he re-lived the year that was passing.

He and his better self were fighting that one great fight—the fight that every man must win or lose—that never-ending battle between "The way that seems the easiest" and "The way that leads to things worth while."

His life seemed full of failures. What a mess he had made of it all! From a place high up in the affairs of men he had laughed at the words of those who were wiser than he. He had frittered away all the words of those who were wiser than he. He had frittered away all that he had gained, trying to buy success with the coin of past achievements.

And, at the beginning of the New Year he was slowly making his way to the top of the mountain where lived a philosopher who was very old and very wise. For many years this man of wisdom had studied the stars and the world below him. He knew the secrets of nature and the works of the wise men of all ages. From all these and from the stones and trees and flowers he had learned the secret of success. To him the young man came for counsel.

"Father," said the youth, "I have come that you may teach me the laws of life. Tell me the secret of success that I may go again among my fellows."

Slowly the old philosopher arose and, pointing to the city far below him, said:

"I have seen the changes wrought by many years; I have seen the miracles of time and to youth I give the secret of it all:

"Make the most of all that comes and the least of all that goes."

What is your attitude as you step from one year into another? Are you looking ahead with confidence or are you looking backward with regret? Think it over—for your success may hinge on your decision at the start.

Don't turn back into the pages of the year that has gone and mourn over things that "might have been." Close the book. Bury it! The blotted pages have done their harm and it is time that they themselves were blotted out.

Don't base your goal on some half-failure of the past, but on some big success of the future. It is not what you have that counts, but what you *expect to have.* Expect much, make sure of your ground—and much you will receive.

Hope

Napoleon Hill

"Do the thing and you shall have the power." –Emerson

The way of success is the way of struggle!

Lincoln wrote the greatest speech ever delivered in the English language, on the back of an envelope, a few moments before it was delivered, yet the thought back of that speech was borne of hardship and struggle.

All down the road of life you will meet with obstacles, many of them. Failure will overtake you time after time, but remember that it is a part of Nature's method to place obstacles and failure in your way, as hurdles are placed before a horse that is being trained, that you may learn from these, some of the greatest of all lessons.

Every time you master failure you become stronger and better prepared to meet the next one. The moments of trial will come to you as they come to all at one time or another. Doubt and lack of faith in yourself and in your fellowmen will cast their dark shadows over you, but remember that the manner in which you react under these trying negatives will indicate whether you are developing the power or slipping backward.

"And this, too, will soon pass away." Nothing is permanent, therefore why permit disappointment, resentment or a keen sense of injustice to undermine your composure, because they will soon eliminate themselves.

Look back over your past and you will see that those experiences of yesterday which bore heavily on your heart at the time, and seemed to end all hope of success, passed away and left you wiser than you were before.

The whole universe is in a constant state of flux. You are in a constant state of change. Evolution is removing the wounds left in your heart by disappointment. You need not go down under any difficulty if you but bear in mind that "this, too, will soon pass away."

I looked back at my heavy load of grief and worry which crowded the happiness out of my heart only yesterday, and lo! They had been transformed into stepping stones of experience over which I had climbed higher and higher.

Source: *Napoleon Hill's Magazine*. September, 1921, p. 9.

What Is Within Us Creates What Is Around Us

Rev. Dr. Sam Boys

It has been said, "Where the mind goes—energy flows." Where we choose to focus our attention and set our intention determines everything else. It is our state of mind—our attitude—that can lead us to success or to failure. We are the makers of our own reality. We are the ones who determine what we manifest in our lives. As we think—so we are. This short story, "The Prophet," serves as a powerful metaphor for our state of mind whenever we set out to accomplish a goal.

The story begins with a young man embarking on his goal of climbing a steep and treacherous mountain. As he climbs, he stumbles and struggles along the way—feeling defeated. His mind seems to be fixed not on the goal of the summit, but on his past failures. He struggles to overcome a past that cannot be changed. The battle he is fighting is within himself. It's the perennial inner struggle between the Big Self and the Small Self, and this inner struggle becomes manifested outwardly and causes him much grief. He sees his life as a failure.

Then, at the beginning of a New Year, he slowly makes his way to the top where he meets a wise, old philosopher who knows the mysteries of Nature and the wisdom of the ages. The young man seeks his counsel. The philosopher's words, "Make the most of all that comes and the least of all that goes" teaches us that our attitude is everything. How we think will determine the outcome of any endeavor. It is not the case that the external world already exists 'out there' independent of us, and we are just tossed to and fro by life's circumstances without any choice. Rather, it is what is within us that will create what is around us. It is not the circumstances themselves, but how we perceive them that determine our success or failure. We are the ones who choose moment to moment the experience we will have in our consciousness, and thus will manifest in our lives.

This gives us pause to take a fearless and searching inventory of our own selves. What is our attitude as we journey through this life? What is our attitude as we step from one year into another? From one project to another? What is our frame of mind as we set out toward a specific goal? Do we set out with a positive mental attitude from the beginning? Or do we defeat ourselves by looking at the impossibilities rather than the possibilities? If so, we have already failed before we even begin.

Napoleon Hill's Principles remind us that there are no failures—only temporary setbacks. This must be our attitude if we are to achieve success in any endeavor. We know that fixing our attention on our definite purpose, applying our faith, fanning the flames of our burning desire, focusing our attention, and keeping a positive mental attitude are crucial to achieving success. Moreover, when temporary setbacks occur, Dr. Hill also reminds us to use our controlled attention to "find, examine, and nurture the seed of equivalent benefit that comes with every unhappiness." Defeat will be nothing but a signal for greater and more determined effort. It will be fuel to feed the fires of our willpower. Hill states that a person will also "learn to delve into their memory to examine defeats that occurred before they selected their definite major purpose." Learn from these defeats, then let them go. Next, move forward with vigor, purpose and the wisdom that comes from experience. This makes every moment of life valuable.

This way of being is best reflected in the poem "The Guest House" by Rumi:

> *This being human is a guest house. Every morning a new arrival. A joy, a depression, a meanness, some momentary awareness comes as an unexpected visitor. Welcome and entertain them all! Even if they're a crowd of sorrows, who violently sweep your house empty of its furniture, still, treat each guest honorably. He may be clearing you out for some new delight. The dark thought, the shame, the malice, meet them at the door laughing, and invite them in. Be grateful for whoever comes, because each has been sent as a guide from beyond.*

Winkers at the Truth

George Harrison Phelps

There are a lot of business men who are cowards. They'd like to know the truth about their business, but they are afraid—or too neglectful—to discover it. They would rather drift fearfully on, trusting to God and Luck.

It's an old trait.

We'd rather worry about unknown ills than undergo the uncertain terrors of a physical examination.

We'd rather let our teeth decay than learn what the dentist's probe may disclose.

We put up with the stain on the ceiling for fear the carpenter will prescribe a re-shingling of the roof.

We fear bad news, even when it's a blessing. We hate it, even when it's a timely warning.

The ancient kings who used to kill the bringers of bad news must have been very foolish, we say.

And then we bar the door to couriers just as important.

A few years ago there was a great mercantile house in New York City. Its name was a household word the world over. Its solvency was as unquestioned as the integrity of those who controlled its destinies.

And then one night the great house crumpled in ruin.

Over its toast and coffee the business world paused in amazement. The news was almost too astounding to be true.

Was anything safe then? Could anyone be trusted?

The auditors gave the answer.

They found no graft—no speculation—no embezzlement—no dishonor. *But*—

They found that the Board of Directors had repeatedly closed its eyes and ears to sounds of warning.

There was a leak in the dike. Everybody had been honest, but nobody had dared expose the thing that for years had been eating at the vitals of the firm.

They had been able to produce millions of dollars of business, but they had feared to throw the spotlight on the truth.

If they hadn't been afraid of Truth, Truth might have saved them.

Don't trust to Luck to bring you through.

Know how your business stands all the time.

If you know there is a rotten spot in it anywhere—face the truth and clean it up.

Just as decay attracts decay in nature—so will it undermine the strongest institution.

These are days when we must be honest with ourselves.

Don't be afraid of the truth.

Squared Accounts

Napoleon Hill

Twelve years ago I enjoyed the acquaintance of a banker, in Washington, D.C. This man began as a dentist and fortune seemed to smile upon him. He began the business of loaning money, in small amounts, at exorbitant rates, as a side issue. He became so successful at this that he finally organized a bank and was elected as its president. This gave him greater prestige and additional financial power, so he began to reach out and buy up real estate, taking a heavy toll from every transaction. The people began to complain of his usurious rates of interest and his tightfisted business methods, but from all outside appearances he continued to gather power and prosper.

I was a client of this man's bank. When I needed money he loaned it to me, but his rates of interest to me were always moderate and in keeping with the rates charged at other banks. I often wondered why he was so fair and liberal with me while he was so unfair and exacting with others. I owned a prosperous School of Mechanical Engineering. I learned, by and by, why this banker was so liberal with me. He wanted that school, and he finally got it. When he had loaned money to me so that he knew I was over my head in the case of an emergency call, he closed me out.

That transaction was a blow to me, *yet, in the light of subsequent years' experience, I know that it was a blessing in disguise;* probably one of the greatest that ever came my way, because it forced me out of a business which played no part in developing strong moral fiber, or laying the foundation for a world-wide service to my fellowmen such as I am rendering today.

I could not prove that this temporary failure was a deliberate part of a great plan to direct my efforts into more constructive channels, but if some power had been putting such a plan into operation it could not have been more successfully conducted than it was. That which was taken away from me ten years ago has been more than repaid within the last three or four years. The Law of Compensation has squared accounts with me, and still the reward seems to be coming my way.

Source: *Napoleon Hill's Magazine.* April, 1921, p. 11.

Don't Be Afraid of the Truth

Mary Akers

I think the last line of this little essay, "Don't be afraid of the truth," is another way of expressing Napoleon Hill's 10th Lesson of Success: Accurate Thinking.

Accurate thinkers don't let anyone else do their thinking for them. Instead, they listen intently, gather the facts, analyze them, and make their own decisions. And accurate thinkers especially don't allow that powerful nemesis of accurate thinking—Fear—to influence their decision-making process. Allowing Fear to think for you is not thinking at all. It is reacting to an imagined, unfortunate event that hasn't even happened yet, and in all likelihood (when accurate thinking is applied to the problem) never will happen.

So, how do we combat fear when making decisions? The simplest way is to first separate fact from fiction—and be sure to keep the facts! Discard the fictions that obfuscate the truth and clutter the decision-making path. Then, once you have your facts, further separate them into two groups: those that are important and those that are unimportant. Unimportant facts are most likely to impede good judgment. If the old expression "Just the Facts, Jack" could be wedded to the ever-useful "Keep It Simple Stupid" we would have an excellent exhortation to provide a clear path for accurate thinking and sound decision-making.

So, learn from the mistakes of the businessmen in this little essay—those men who buried their heads in the sand like ostriches as threat approached and thereby lost everything. Instead of ignoring reality, keep your head up, assemble the facts (yes, even the unpleasant ones), analyze and sort them, and then all of your decisions will become informed decisions. After all, if you don't know, you can't act. And it's always better to take decisive action now than to be forced to simply react to adverse circumstances later.

The Cursing Post

George Harrison Phelps

Intelligent co-operation is the life of business. Boost and the world is with you. Knock and you go alone. Persist in using your little hammer on your next-door neighbor and you automatically take the greased slide to oblivion.

Everywhere of late years the conviction has been growing that we must treat the other fellow fairly, as we expect to be treated in turn. For 1900 years we have tried every other way. Now we are beginning to realize that only absolute squareness goes. The golden rule never tarnishes.

Still, there are salesmen who haven't yet realized that this is true. They sometimes deliberately emphasize the supposedly weak points of the other fellow's product; they run down rival companies. And all the time they are tightening the noose about their own necks. They fill the mind of the buyer with hatred, distrust and fear. They throw a scare into him. Instead of putting him in a contented, buying mood, they give him gooseflesh.

In this way the misguided one creates a negative atmosphere. He loses the customer's confidence—by far the greatest factor in any sale. His action, however, has a more vital and far-reaching effect. *He hits his own business future below the belt.*

My old friend Thomas Drier used to rave and rant when he met a knocker. Usually, on calming down, he would tell the story of the youth who cursed like a Black Sea pirate until, one day, his father led him into the yard and said:

"Look, son, at this fine new post that has been set solidly in the ground. This is your property. Whenever you feel like cursing, and do curse—and you have my permission to curse as much as you please—I want you to drive a nail into this post. And, whenever you repress a desire to curse, I want you to pull a nail out of the post."

The son entered into the spirit of the game and soon found that the post was filled with nails, until it resembled an angry porcupine. He became a bit ashamed, and began to resist temptations to express himself in lurid language. Whenever he resisted successfully, he pulled out a nail.

Eventually every nail had been withdrawn and with some pride he summoned his father.

"It is fine, my son," commented the old man, "but there is still one thing you must do, if you would leave the post as you found it ... you must pull out the holes left by the nails."

Tolerance

Napoleon Hill

If you must slander someone do not speak it, but, write it; write it in the sand, near the water's edge.

When the dawn of Intelligence shall have spread its wings over the Eastern horizon of progress, and Ignorance and Superstition shall have left their last footprints on the sands of Time, it will be recorded in the book of man's crimes that his most grievous since was that of Intolerance.

The bitterest Intolerance grows out of racial and religious differences of opinion. How long, O Master of Human Destinies, until we poor mortals will understand the folly of trying to destroy one another?

Our allotted time of this earth is but a fleeting moment, at most!

Like a candle, we are lighted, shine for a few moments and flicker out! Why can we not so live during this short earthly sojourn that when the Great Caravan called Death draws up and announces this visit about finished we will be ready to fold our tents, and, like the Arabs of the Desert, silently follow the Caravan out into the Great Unknown without fear or trembling?

I am hoping that I will find no Jews or Gentiles, Catholics or Protestants, Germans or Englishmen, French or Russians, Whites or Blacks, when I shall have crossed the Bar to the other side.

I am hoping I shall find there only human souls, Brothers and Sisters all; unmarked by race, creed or color, for I shall want to be done with Intolerance, so I may lie down and rest an aeon or two, undisturbed by the petty strife and chaos and misunderstandings which too often mark this earthly existence.

O, Infinite Intelligence, connect me with the Universal source of Wisdom and common sense, so I may be tolerant with my fellowmen as I tarry by the wayside of life.

Source: *On Top O'The World. A Personal Statement by Napoleon Hill.* November 11, 1918, back cover.

The Holes Remain

Fr. Bob Sipe

In the days when I was a parish priest we used to use a questionnaire with couples preparing for marriage that helped them reflect on their differences and similarities. It included questions about money, in-laws, common interests, religion, communication styles, and conflict resolution. There was one question that most couples found very difficult to answer. It was this: "If my partner were ever unfaithful would it mean the end of our marriage?"

Usually, after a long pause, the idealistic ones would say, "Well, that could never happen to us." Others, to break the ice with a little humor might say something like, "It sure would, I'd kill him (her)." I would usually follow up with questions, sometimes playing the Devil's Advocate.

"Why would you be so upset? It's only sex. What's a poor boy to do when some dumb broad throws her keys at him, or some handsome and understanding guy really listens to a girl when she is feeling down? Everyone is doing it, just listen to the talk shows. Besides, you two are living together and having sex and you are not married, so what's the big deal?"

After a lengthy discussion it would come out that either or both would be deeply wounded by an affair, and while forgiveness might come, it might take a long time for the wound to heal, if ever. And that has been my experience in my fifty years in the priesthood. People can forgive a betrayal of trust, but the wound remains, and the level of trust is seldom ever the same. You can pull out the nails, but the holes remain.

Admiral Dewey

George Harrison Phelps

It matters little who we are or what we do. At the bottom of the ladder or at the top, we must answer the command of the ranking officer. Every man needs supervision. It makes no difference what his work, monarch of money or moulder of clay.

There is always someone above who knows. Someone is competent to give command. It's only the little man who can't take orders. It's the pigmy who refuses to listen.

When his country paused to mourn the death of its great naval hero, few remembered that Admiral George Dewey was in Manila Bay on that memorable Sunday morning in '98, not because he believed it the place to be, but because he was under orders—because he was big enough to obey, even against his better judgment.

For several months the United States had been preparing for the coming clash with Spain. It seemed inevitable. Eager to serve his country with the best at his command, Dewey looked forward to a position of importance in the conflict. They, in the height of his anticipation, he received an order to sail for the Far East at once.

For the first time in his long career as a naval officer, Dewey rebidded—within himself. He felt the sting of discrimination. He thoroughly believed he was being "shelved." His own best judgment told him that the decisive battles of the war with Spain would be fought in Cuban waters—and he, with his

Pacific squadron, would be twirling his thumbs on the other side of the globe.

It was the most critical moment of his life and he wavered between duty and distrust.

But discipline and a mind broad enough to admit the superiority of those who stood above him proved the deciding influence.

Unlike Achilles, he refused to sulk. He obeyed.

The battle of Manila Bay was one of the most remarkable in the history of modern warfare. Disastrous to the Spanish, it was an almost bloodless triumph for the Stars and Stripes. Dewey at once became his nation's idol. Strange, how we often battle and rebel today against the things we will want and need tomorrow.

Be big enough to obey.

Be a soldier.

"Ich Dien" (I Serve)

Napoleon Hill

Work thou for pleasure; paint or sing or carve
The thing thou lovest, though the body starve.
Who works for glory misses oft the goal.
Who works for money coins his very soul.
Work for work's sake then, and it well may be
That these things shall be added unto thee.

The Prince of Wales has adopted as his motto, "Ich Dien," meaning, "I Serve." If he applies his motto literally he can become a useful leader instead of a useless prince.

About three score years ago two men were contestants for the presidency of the United States. One was polished, schooled, clever in the use of words and adept in the strategy of politics. The other was unschooled, droll in manner, and unfamiliar with the cunning of politicians. Douglas, the highly developed intellectual type, but devoid of emotion. Lincoln, whose heart always registered the emotions of the common people.

Douglas wanted the presidency that the people might have greater opportunity to serve him. Lincoln wanted the presidency that he might have greater opportunity to serve the people.

History clearly records that which followed. Today Douglas is all but forgotten, while the spirit of Lincoln will go marching on forever. It pays to serve. It pays to keep faith with those whom one pledges his sacred world of honor to serve. Neither poverty nor lowly birth can permanently withhold success from the person whose motto is, "Ich Dien," if he lives up to his motto.

Whether your calling takes you into the mire of ditch digging or places upon shoulders the responsibility of providing a pay-roll for hundreds of men and managing a great industry, you will be appropriately rewarded if you serve well. If you live to serve you cannot fail; if you live only to be served your doom is sealed in advance.

You can pattern yourself after either Douglas or Lincoln. Take your choice.

Fortunate is the person who renders more service and better service than is paid for, because that person is sure to be paid, sooner or later, for more service than is actually rendered.

Source: *Napoleon Hill's Magazine*. October, 1921, p. 13.

Acta Non Verba

Joe Stewart, Vice Admiral USMS (ret)

While the essay on Admiral Dewey is for me an interesting and thought provoking piece, I found it a bit challenging to relate it to the teachings of Napoleon Hill. Moreover, I don't think Napoleon Hill would agree with the essay's first sentence—"It matters little who we are or what we do." On the other hand, if he were alive today, I believe Hill would say individuals are defined by how they embrace and practice his principles of personal success. Who we are and what we do matters. The Admiral Dewey article seems to focus on supervision and the importance of obedience; however, Napoleon Hill's teachings, in my view, go far beyond the concept of following orders. When exercised, Hill's principles would create in one the capacity to be a good soldier, to subordinate oneself to the overall mission and to get the job done with initiative and a positive mental attitude. I believe these are some of the attributes that lead to Dewey's success at Manila Bay. In other words, the Admiral did a lot more than just obeying his orders.

My theory is that Admiral Dewey was victorious at Manila Bay not only because he did as he was ordered, but because he was a leader who used the Hill teaching of controlled attention to focus on the mission that was assigned to him. Certainly, Napoleon Hill recognized that we all have a boss. Additionally, I think he would have wanted us to be big enough to obey honorable orders. Nevertheless, his principles are bigger than obedience.

Many years ago as a plebe at the U S Naval Academy I was required to read a short book that's had a real impact on my life. The title is *A Message to Garcia.* It's about obeying your leader, and it came to mind when reading the Admiral Dewey essay. It also reminds me of the magnificent motto of the U.S. Merchant Marine Academy—*"Acta Non Verba"—deeds not words*. I'm convinced this motto, Deeds not Words, was embraced by Admiral Dewey and would be one that Napoleon Hill would have liked.

A Message to Garcia is also about the Spanish American War and describes the initiative, obedience, and *acta non verba* attitude of an Army major who is tasked by President McKinley to deliver a letter to General Garcia, the leader of the Cuban insurgents. Major Rowan took the letter without asking where General Garcia was or how he was to get there. In four days he landed off the coast of Cuba in an open boat, traversed a hostile jungle territory for three weeks and delivered the President's letter. Major Rowan obeyed President McKinley just as Admiral Dewey obeyed his superior officer. They both were successful. Several of Napoleon Hill's teachings must have been followed.

In my view, the two most significant points of the Admiral Dewey essay that relate specifically to Napoleon Hill's teachings are first that success is inevitable when teamwork is the dominating influence. I'm convinced that Admiral Dewey believed in service to the United States and understood that unselfishly placing the mission above his personal interests would lead to victory. And second, that developing positive habits influences one's thoughts. Our thoughts influence our actions which then lead to success. I believe Admiral Dewey did the right thing because he had developed positive thoughts. Following orders had become a habit and the Admiral had become a good soldier.

Health

George Harrison Phelps

I have just stumbled onto an old letter written to me some years ago by a pal of mine. It breathes such a wealth of vigor and sunshine and fresh air and new life that I want to pass it on to you just the way he wrote it. Perhaps it will help you to stop your patter-patter in the worry mill, and to get out in the open where everything in nature seems to be starting life anew.

"I suppose it's the spring," he wrote; "I can't account for it in any other way. Like the young birds, I want to fly. You, evidently, are feeling the same urge. Last night the desire came to me to go out and hustle with physical work for a few months. I know that is what I need. I know that we must all get away from continually thinking the same kind of thoughts. You remember the fairy story of the man whose strength was renewed every time he touched the earth. I would like to imitate him and get close to the ground for a little while.

"It would be good to know what it means to work until the honest sweat pours out. Just to have the appetite that was once mine, when I worked in a sawmill—that would be the finest kind of joy.

"Of course, it takes courage to change. I sometimes envy the real vagabonds—the fellows who have the courage to migrate. I know that every time a fellow moves he loses something. But it is also possible that every time he moves he gains something that is worth far more than that which he lost.

"This spring feeling makes me tired of familiar things and familiar people. Right now I'd like to don some rough clothes and hit the trail. Maybe I will. It would be fine to quit this worry and fuss and go out in the open air and live for a while. What you and I need is Health.

"It doesn't make a damn bit of difference how much fame and money we get if we don't have health. And we cannot have health by mixing life with fret and worry. The body must be exercised. The brain, too, needs exercise in the form of new and refreshing thought. Right now, for instance, just to show my contempt for work and for the office, I'm going to take a tramp around Fresh Water Pond."

This man knows how to live. He knows that to increase one's income it is necessary to increase the quality and quantity of one's output. To do this the human machine must be kept in good repair. It must be overhauled and brightened up.

Prove it to yourself—get out now—take a day off—and see what a difference it will make.

Solitude

Napoleon Hill

Tempest-tossed souls, wherever ye may be,
under whatsoever conditions ye may live,
know this—in the ocean of life the isles of
Blessedness are smiling, and the sunny
shore of your ideal awaits your coming.
Keep your hand firmly on the helm of
thought. In the bark of your soul reclines
the commanding Master. Wake him.

Get away from the crowds, relax, quit the business of thing, and give the genius within you a chance to express itself. Thirty minutes a day devoted to relaxation will give you poise and self-control, without which you can never become a master in any undertaking.

There is something in the calm stillness of nature which gives one faith, courage and self-confidence. Go out into the woods, away from everybody, and give the subtle forces of nature a chance to lay hold on you.

In the solitude of your own heart, during these visits with your inner self, you will learn who you are and what your mission in life is.

Milton did his greatest work after blindness forced him to seek his inner self as a companion. Helen Keller has become the marvel of this age because she was deprived of the senses of sight, hearing and speech and was forced to seek companionship with her inner self.

The connecting link between you and God may be found within your own heart, and nowhere else. There is a secret passageway between you and mastery, and it can be discovered only through that calm sereneness of thought which will flow in on you when you are alone, relaxed and receptive.

This is no mere preachment, but a scientific truth, which, if studied and applied, may bead you upward to the heights of your desires.

> *Every man is where he is by the law of his being; the thoughts which he has built into his character have brought him there, and in the arrangement of his life there is no element of chance, but all is the result of a law which cannot err.*

Source: *Napoleon Hill's Magazine*. July, 1921, p. 15.

A Healthy Practice

Uriel "Chino" Martinez

Infusing fresh ideas into our thinking can be as easy as stepping out doors and enjoying our natural surroundings. Taking a deep breath of fresh air and engaging in some kind of physical activity can spark a new idea. Spring time in the Northern Midwest of the United States is a very welcomed season after months of being confined in our indoor habitat with the naturally diminished daylight. Spring marks the lengthening of our daylight hours and everything begins to come to life with the blooming of nature.

Patterns in nature have been a curiosity studied by man to bring order to his existence. A pattern of unknown origins, inspired by nature and known as the labyrinth has been passed on from generation to generation and found across the entire earth. This pattern has evolved with man over 4,000 years. It is a pattern that can be walked, in fact the most famous labyrinth pattern is found in the confines of a thirteenth century cathedral in Chartres, France. Surprisingly, this confining and beautiful pattern has a way of helping us breakout of our everyday thinking and frees us to ever more complex and new patterns of thought. The labyrinth is a metaphor for our own life's journey. Twisting and turning it takes us into each quadrant like the pattern of the wind and the passing of the seasons. It has been said that we think 70,000 thoughts a day, but the issue is that they are the same thoughts. The labyrinth can be a metaphorical representation of a pattern of thought, a new pattern that you have not yet tread. Being physically engaged in walking this pattern prompts the mind to the possibility of new thought patterns.

The thought pattern of worrying is the greatest loss of energy. It is as useless as the unharnessed power of the wind lost forever. But on the contrary, engaging our minds in an active positive meditation is like constructing many windmills and capturing the power of the wind to light up thousands of homes in rural Indiana, USA. Nobel Prize winner Dr. Ilya Prigogine would call a windmill a "dissipative structure." He indicated that all of nature and the fruits and vegetables that are produced from the wide variety of plants are entities that have created something out of resources that would otherwise have been lost.

To me the labyrinth is such a dissipative structure that through the ordinary act of walking and engaging our mind in meditation, we can become more creative through the good use of our time which otherwise would be lost.

Our busy lives can disrupt the mind body spirit connection that insures us a full life. Science is ever confirming the mind body spirit connection. New ideas come not only from our thinking but from our moving or taking action and from Infinite Intelligence. I encourage you to walk an outdoor labyrinth in mindful meditation to enhance your subconscious mind. Learn to listen to your heart, your head, your body and your spirit. It is when you pause and reflect in this particular meditation that you are more open to recalling or withdrawing thoughts from the subconscious mind, *"as letters may be taken from a filing cabinet"* as Napoleon Hill states in *Think and Grow Rich*.

Discover a labyrinth near you by using the labyrinth locator found at LabyrinthSociety.org. If for the moment you cannot access a labyrinth, find a path in a park or the woods that can serve as a virtual labyrinth.

Safe at Second

George Harrison Phelps

Achievement is just as much of a habit as failing. The man who gets the habit of overcoming obstacles with cheerfulness and determination, soon ceases to call them obstacles.

He takes pride in achieving those things which others fear.

Accomplishment of the difficult is the thing that takes the humdrum out of business.

Once get the habit of finishing what you start, and your own progress will astonish you.

You won't be able to fail.

Thomas Dreier tells a story of Detroit's own inimitable Ty Cobb that illustrates this. "The Tigers were playing in New York, and secured so many runs that the crowd has lost all interest in the game. Near the end of the last inning Cobb was on first. 'Step off and let them tag you out, Ty. For Heaven's sake, finish it,' said Bill Donovan, who was coaching near first. Ty grinned and stepped from the bag, his hands at his sides, waiting to be tagged. The catcher shot the ball to first, and right there at that moment the crowd saw a bit of the most sensational base-running in the history of baseball.

"Ty tried to stand still and be tagged. But his training, his habit of succeeding, his ability to finish what he started, and his ambition to overcome his opponent, proved too strong for him. He zig-zagged back and forth with the whole infield chasing him. Finally someone threw a trifle wild, and in a fraction of a second Ty had made one of his famous dives that landed him in a whirl of dust, safe at second.

"'Why didn't you let them tag you out as you agreed?' he was asked after the game.

"'Well, I started to, all right,' he answered, 'but gee whiz! after I stood there a second and saw that ball coming, I simply couldn't do it. I said, By jiminy, if you fellows get me, you'll have to work for it. *I Just Couldn't Stand Still and Let Them Tag Me Out Without Making a Fight.*'"

The Looking Glass

Napoleon Hill

No matter how many friends prove false and thereby strike a blow at your confidence in others, there is always one person to whom you can turn for consolation in hours of trial and disappointment.

You may see this person by stepping to the looking glass!

And, after all has been said and done there is no one on whom you need to rely and who is more able to help you, than yourself. It may serve as an alibi if you blame your failures on others, but the truth will remain that you, yourself, are responsible for your advancement or lack of it, and you are indeed fortunate if you get this consciousness and henceforth hold yourself accountable for your condition in life.

Make excuses for the shortcomings of OTHERS, but hold YOURSELF to strict accountability if you would attain leadership in any undertaking.

Source: *Napoleon Hill's Magazine*. July, 1921, inside back cover.

Patience

George Harrison Phelps

True faith in a deserving man or a deserving institution is an invisible force which works quietly and surely for the good of that toward which it is directed. Every individual and every organization must have the faith of their associates. True faith recognizes the inevitable disappointments and meets them unflinchingly. It sees only sincerity and firmness of purpose for the ultimate success of all.

Hardly a day came without some inspirational example from overseas. Early in the war a division of French troops was saved from annihilation because its commander had the true faith of a soldier.

The division had opened an attack upon the enemy, who was entrenched in a Gibraltar-like position on a distant knoll. The assault had carried well and the French had succeeded in dislodging the foremost German lines. The way to victory seemed reasonably certain.

As the troops started off on the second charge, a great mountain of earth and flame belched up with a mighty roar, annihilating half of the forces and leaving a gaping abyss of death between the ranks in the front and rear. A German mine had been let go at a crucial moment.

Panic gripped the hearts of the men who now stood trembling and hesitant between the advancing enemy in front and the smoldering breach of death behind them. The commander's first humane impulse was to order a retreat, but he remembered that this particular position was the pivotal point of a great and decisive engagement. It must be taken at any cost.

He knew what the fate of his men would be unless some almost miraculous intervention should come to their aid. And then he thought of that little sheltered cottage far behind the lines where great men and great minds were calmly directing and planning every move and position of a million men. He knew that modern science had made it possible for the generals who guide the destinies of battle, to keep in instant touch with every development.

He ordered the fragment of his command to charge. Their numbers were ridiculously out of proportion with the enemy's. But his faith was great enough to even the balance.

Fired by his own courage in the face of these odds, his men fought with furious determination. The hand-to-hand conflict dragged on and the lines grew thinner and thinner. Human endurance was almost at an end. Faith and patience began a mighty struggle.

Then suddenly great streams of men poured over the broken hill and around the chasm of death. It had seemed hours since the German mine exploded, but in reality just twelve minutes after telegraphic information of the disaster reached the generals in the secluded cottage the reinforcements had turned defeat into victory.

Faith and Daring had won.

In the parallel incidents of your own daily work strive to conduct yourself with the patient forbearance of the French commander. Stifle your disappointments. Put your faith in the man or institution from whom you expect your reinforcements. You will feel firm assurance of fair play and ultimate victory.

Have Faith.

No Substitute for Persistence

Napoleon Hill

Those who can "take it" are bountifully rewarded for their PERSISTENCE. They receive, as their compensation, whatever goal they are pursuing. This is not all! They receive something infinitely more important than material compensation—the knowledge that "EVERY FAILURE BRINGS WITH IT THE SEED OF AN EQUIVALENT ADVANTAGE."

There are exceptions to this rule; a few people know from experience the soundness of persistence. They are the ones who have not accepted defeat as being anything more than temporary. They are the ones whose DESIRES are so PERSISTENTLY APPLIED that defeat is finally changed into victory. We who stand on the side-lines of Life see the overwhelmingly large number who go down in defeat, never to rise again. We see the few who take the punishment of defeat as an urge to greater effort. These, fortunately, never learn to accept Life's reverse gear. But what we DO NOT SEE, what most of us never suspect of existing, is the silent but irresistible POWER which comes to the rescue of those who fight on in the face of discouragement. If we speak of this power at all we call it PERSISTENCE, and let it go at that. One thing we all know, if one does not possess PERSISTENCE, one does not achieve noteworthy success in any calling.

Source: *Think and Grow Rich.* The Ralston Society, 1937, p 230.

Patience: Definiteness of Purpose

Gail Brooks

The French Commander had a definite purpose. He was on a mission. The position he and his men were fighting to secure was a pivotal point in defeating the Germans—and victory seemed imminent. Then, suddenly, adversity of catastrophic proportions struck! A German mine had been let go at a crucial moment and panic gripped the hearts of the French soldiers standing between the enemy and the smoldering trench behind them.

But, the Commander also had faith. Faith in the great men and great minds that were sheltered in the little cottage behind the lines. He had faith in the modern science at the disposal of those Generals and in their ability to guide the destinies of battle.

In spite of the adversity he and his men faced, the French Commander remembered the importance of this particular position. He remembered his purpose. The knoll the French Commander was fighting to secure had to be taken at any cost—even at the cost of his life and the lives of his men. He was driven to action by the knowledge of his purpose fueled by his faith giving him the strength and resolve required to overcome the adversity he and his men faced.

According to Dr. Napoleon Hill, faith is a state of mind. It is the ability to believe you have won before you have. It's the art of beating the enemy, the obstacles, or the plan of your opponents. Faith is the believing you will be victorious before the battle begins.

Dr. Hill teaches us that the greatest benefit of definiteness of purpose is that it opens your mind to the quality known as faith.

It makes your mind positive and frees it from the limitations of doubt, discouragement, indecision, and procrastination.

The French Commander had a definite purpose that resulted in a faith that allowed him to believe that he and his men would be victorious in spite of the adversities they faced.

How strong is your belief?

Faith is the essence of every great achievement, no matter what its nature or purpose. For faith to be useful to you in achieving lasting success, it must be active not passive. First, have faith in yourself and your ability to take action to do the next right thing. Then have faith in the thing you set out to do—faith in your definite purpose. Finally, have Faith in the result—an unwavering belief that you will achieve your goals regardless of the adversities or obstacles encountered.

Your success is limited only by your Faith.

Their numbers were out of proportion, but the French Commander's faith was great—great enough to even the balance. Possessing faith in yourself and in the fact that the Universe is constructed to allow you to achieve your greatest potential will help you overcome obstacles, deal positively with negative circumstances and replace fear with courage.

Napoleon Hill says, "Faith helps you see your plans a completed reality, even before you begin putting them into operation." From the beginning of time, all of the great stories of success are about men and women who had faith.

Faith feeds the hungry in adversity and clothes and warms the needy in temporary failure. Faith is a combination of thought and action. Faith builds. It cannot destroy.

Regardless of your circumstances, make faith a vital part of your determination to Win. It will serve you beyond belief.

Bill McQuigg

George Harrison Phelps

There is no such thing as a selling season. Ice and cold or heat and rain are incidentals in the day's work. Successful salesmanship is largely a matter of courage—courage to believe in a bigger and better business than you have ever had—courage to go after it—courage to stick with it.

Let me tell you the story of Bill McQuigg, as told to me by my good friend Ray Clarke Rose, long a star reporter on a Chicago newspaper, and the man who found Bill years ago. The dealer who can lose courage after knowing what Bill McQuigg did—well, he can be little more than a poor excuse for a business man.

"Bill says he doubts if he ever had any backbone until he got his broken some thirteen years ago. From that day to this he has been dead practically from the waist down, and he declares that he really began to live at that moment when you and I, brother salesmen, might have felt justified in giving up and dying. Most chaps do who get their backbone broken across the middle. The most wonderful part of it all is, Bill's optimism is so huge, so virile and brawny that after facing him for five minutes you are inclined rather to envy him and to wonder if it wouldn't be worth your while to go and get your back broken just to make a man of you.

"Listen to what he has done. Purchased a farm for his father and mother; established a successful printing business for himself; purchased valuable real estate in Chicago; developed a glorious cheerfulness that conquers pain that is constant, nearly, and a deathly sickness that clutches him at intervals. Bill lies in his shop, propped up by a mass of pillows, with proof and copy all about him on the bed. Directly in front of him are heaped up ridges of paper stock, as colorful as a mountain sunset. Bill sometimes calls them his mountain peaks of unliberated thought, and he may tell you of the fairies of fancy that comes stealing through the paper presses sometimes during the long nights that he spends there in the heart of the Italian Quarter of Chicago. Bill never leaves his shop. I suppose you insist upon knowing how the accident happened. It really doesn't matter, but he was sinking a shaft in a little gold prospect in Arizona. As he bent forward to light his cigarette a bit of quartz slipped down the shaft and tapped him gently in the small of the back. In a flash Bill was changed from a reckless, hardy adventurer to a despairing, pain-racked and helpless cripple. However, Bill is no hero—he refuses to be lionized. In passing back and forth through the Valley of the Shadow of Death, for his soul's sake he came to believe that power comes to the chap who grits his teeth and wades in."

This is why I say to you, brother salesman, if you imagine that business is slowing up—if it's the "other fellow" who's getting the orders that you should have—if, in fact, you have reached the stage where you are prepared to hibernate and wait again for clear skies and sunny days, pull in your belt and make a little pilgrimage to William H. McQuigg—man and gentleman—and then get back on the job and make the sparks fly upward—Sir.

Breaks Made to Order

Napoleon Hill

Many people believe that material success is the result of favorable "breaks." There is an element of ground for the belief, but those depending entirely upon luck are nearly always disappointed, because they overlook another important factor which must be present before one can be sure of success. It is the knowledge that favorable "breaks" can be made to order.

During the depression, W. C. Fields, the comedian, lost all his money and found himself without income, without a job, and his means of earning a living (vaudeville) no longer existed. Moreover, he was past sixty, when many men consider themselves "old." He was so eager to stage a comeback that he offered to work without pay, in a new field (movies). In addition to his other troubles, he fell and injured his neck. To many that would have been the place to give up and QUIT. But Fields was PERSISTENT. He knew that if he carried on he would get the "breaks" sooner or later, and he did get them, but not by chance.

Source: *Think and Grow Rich*. The Ralston Society, 1937, pp. 238–239.

Haig

George Harrison Phelps

Your business takes its temper from the mood of the man who manages it. The enthusiasm of your employees is never greater than the enthusiasm of the man who directs them. They watch you as you open your desk in the morning. They mark their time by yours.

If you give them courage and hope and enthusiasm they will bring you more and better business. If you give them gloom and war talk and pessimism you will quickly pay for it in loss of sales.

Isaac F. Marcosson, the famous war correspondent, tells a story that will help you when you feel discouraged.

"It was at the beginning of the first battle of Ypres," he writes, "when that immortal thin line of British khaki, bent but not broken, stemmed the mighty German avalanche and blocked the passage to the sea. Outnumbered more than ten to one in some places, it fought with that desperate and dogged tenacity which has always been the inheritance of the British soldier. Every impromptu trench was a Valhalla of English gallantry. Deeds that in other wars would have stood out conspicuously were here merged into an endless succession of deathless glory.

"To the right of Ypres things were going badly. The deluge of German shells was well-nigh unbearable. Even the most heroic courage could not prevail against such an uneven balance of strength. The cry was for men, and yet every man was engaged.

"Now came the event which bound this silent soldier to his men with bands of steel. For twenty-four hours the furies of battle had raged. The German bombardment was now a hideous storm of dripping death. The Prussian Guard rose like magic legions out of the ground. They had just broken through one British line and small parties of khakied troops were in retreat.

"Suddenly down the Menin road, with Ypres silhouetted behind like a mystic city shrouded with smoke, rode Sir Douglas Haig—trim, well groomed, serene, sitting his horse erect and unafraid, and with an escort of his own Seventeenth Lancers as perfectly turned out as on peace parade. Overhead was the incessant shriek of shells, and all around carnage reigned. A thrill of spontaneous admiration swept those tired and battered troops, for the spectacle they beheld was as unlike war as night is unlike day.

"The effect of that calm and confident presence acted like a cooling draught on a parched tongue. It galvanized the waning strength in the gory trenches; the retreat became an advance and the broken line was restored. Haig had turned the tide."

You are the Haig of Your forces. Remember, your men have their eyes on you every minute of the day.

You Can't Afford to Droop.

Leadership

Napoleon Hill

Leadership means responsibilities, but the most profitable work usually is that which shoulders the greatest responsibility on a man.

Wherever there is work to be done you can find a chance to become a leader. It may be humble leadership, at first, but the leadership becomes a habit and soon the most humble leader becomes a powerful man of action and he is then sought for greater leadership.

Look back down the ages and history will tell you that leadership was the quality which thrust greatness upon the men of the past.

Washington, Lincoln, Patrick Henry, Roosevelt, Dewey—leaders, all!

None of these were invited to become leaders. They stepped into leadership by their own aggressiveness. None of them started at the top. Most of them began in the most lowly capacity, but they formed the habit of doing that which needed to be done, whether it was their job to do it or not; whether they were paid for it or not!

If you are one of the great majority who have made up their minds not to do anything which is not their job, and for which they are not paid, there is no hope of leadership crowning your efforts.

James J. Hill was a telegraph operator, but had he delivered no more service than was required to hold the job of telegrapher he doubtless never would have been the great railroad builder that he was.

Leadership! What a wonderful privilege it is to be a leader! What a wonderful opportunity there is in every shop, factory, crossroads grocery store and business establishment, to become a leader by merely doing the thing that ought to be done whether you are told to do it or not.

Source: *Napoleon Hill's Magazine*. April, 1923, inside back cover.

Licking Luck

George Harrison Phelps

The fellow who can transform himself from a physical and almost a mental wreck into a specialist in nervous and mental diseases is my idea of a good man to pattern after. There are a lot of us who need a mental stimulant of some kind. I have noticed it particularly within the last few weeks, when I was trying to impress certain people with the knowledge that they COULD do what they FEARED they COULDN'T do.

James Hay, Jr., tells the story of a man who drifted farther and farther from success with every year of his life. As a college student he became a "bad luck" believer. He was "unlucky" as a physician, and after four years he quit. He bought a drug store. Three years later he failed again. The phantom misfortune could not be shaken.

Heartsick and still cursing his "luck," he became a prescription clerk in an all-night drug store. His pride was shattered. His energy was gone. "Luck" was not with him. He had the makings of a successful man, but the "breaks" were against him.

During the long hours of idleness in the store at night he fell into the habit of reading books that had to do with nervous and mental diseases. Their philosophy naturally appealed to him. Then one night he suddenly realized that he was crammed with knowledge on the subject. It was his chance to come back. He made up his mind that from this last remnant of hope he would weave the fabric of a permanent success.

He went to see a famous nerve specialist whom he had known in his early practice. He told him what he knew about the influence of worry on the nervous make-up. He told him about the terrific amount of mental suffering and nerve strain caused by the habit people had of concealing their trouble and refusing to confide in their physicians.

"You have your bromides, your electrical treatments and your hypnotism," he said. "Now, I'm offering you a fourth element—the application of real psychology to those of your patients who need it, my analysis of their suffering and my enlightenment of them so that they may live their lives properly and be well, normal persons. You dose them—and I'll talk to them, teach them the absurdity of fear."

He was able to convince the specialist because he had lived the philosophy he now proposed to teach.

A few months later he was a specialist himself in nervous and mental diseases. He had managed to lose all interest in the question of luck. The bad luck bogey had vanished in thin air forever. Today he enjoys a lucrative practice. He is an optimistic, self-reliant man.

And this is why he says there is no such thing as bad luck. Bad luck is nothing but bad work. A man's misfortunes are really nothing but his mistakes. If there is ever a "curse" on him it is entirely the curse of his own cowardice. To believe in bad luck is a beautiful excuse for failure. It is a perfect defense against hard work. If you have a premonition that you are going to fail in an undertaking, you are promising yourself disaster in advance.

Dismiss the premonitions. Throw away the "charm" and the talismans. GET ON THE JOB!

The Seven Major Negative Emotions (To Be Avoided)

Napoleon Hill

- The emotion of FEAR
- The emotion of JEALOUSY
- The emotion of HATRED
- The emotion of REVENGE
- The emotion of GREED
- The emotion of SUPERSTITION
- The emotion of ANGER

Positive and negative emotions cannot occupy the mind at the same time. One or the other must dominate. It is your responsibility to make sure that positive emotions constitute the dominating influence of your mind. Here the law of HABIT will come to your aid. Form the habit of applying and using the positive emotions! Eventually, they will dominate your mind so completely, that the negatives cannot enter it.

Source: *Think and Grow Rich*. The Ralston Society, 1937, pp. 297–298.

Licking Luck Does Not Equal Accurate Thinking

Dr. J.B. Hill

Although Napoleon Hill wrote extensively about the principles of success, he must have been equally conversant with the contrasting reasons for failure. Since he did not include "Luck" as one of his principles of success, he could hardly consider "bad luck" as a precursor to failure. To Dr. Hill, good luck was merely an opportunity presenting itself to someone prepared to take advantage of it. Bad luck was nothing more than an alibi.

In *Think and Grow Rich,* Napoleon wrote that "there is a difference between WISHING for a thing and being READY for it." I am reminded of the story of the man that paid $50,000 for property during a quick cash sale. A week later, he was able to sell it for twice what he paid. Was he lucky? Or was he READY to take advantage of an opportunity that came his way because he had saved the money he needed to buy the property?

If luck is not a principle for success, can it still be a reason for failure? Many think so because luck is a convenient culprit residing somewhere beyond our control. It is used to explain failure to others but it is much more likely to be used to excuse failure to ourselves. Dr. Hill named 57 common excuses, which he called alibis: "If I only got a break; if I had been born rich; etc." Every alibi implicitly involves luck and every alibi describes a condition seemingly outside the control of its holder. Bad luck is the perfect alibi for failure. Luck apparently depends on how we think about it.

One of Dr. Hill's principles of success is to form the habit of accurate thinking. He writes that the accurate thinker separates fact from fiction. Accurate thinking leads to understanding that luck is a random event. We can and do protect ourselves as best we can against its random nature. For example, we purchase insurance, diversify investments, broaden product lines, take safe guards, and avoid risks—all to temper the effects of random adversity. When adversity comes, and it always does, accurate thinking has prepared us to deal with it and to surmount it.

Licking luck is not that difficult. It just requires us to think accurately about it. We have to be ready to take advantage of opportunity and we have to think ahead to take steps that will lessen the effects of, well … bad luck.

D. C. Jackling

George Harrison Phelps

Making up your mind to begin the battle is half the game; nerve to stick to the finish is the other half. Perhaps you have read of D. C. Jackling. Jackling fought his battle in rounds. He went fresh into every one and made up his mind when he started that he was going through.

At eighteen he was a teamster on a farm, making fifteen dollars a month. He heard that the teacher in the district school was getting thirty dollars, so he at once determined to become a teacher. It was the biggest salary he'd ever heard of. Presently the teacher took a job in a hardware store in the city at seventy-five a month. Jackling at once saw bigger opportunities in the city and went there. In Sedalia, Mo., he saw a civil engineer at work with his transit. Never before had he seen one, but he was curious. The moment he learned that the engineer made one hundred dollars a month he determined to follow in his footsteps. He worked his way through the Missouri School of Mines.

Through just such adversities, Jackling climbed—higher and higher, each time tackling the next round with a firm determination to go through. That is why, at the age of thirty, he was a mine superintendent at three thousand dollars a year; at thirty-five, vice-president and general manager of a mining company; at forty, a millionaire; at forty-seven—his age today—a multi-millionaire controlling the operation of four great mines.

It was at thirty-five that Jackling showed the mettle that made the man. Delegated by his employer to report on the advisability of reopening an abandoned copper mine in Utah, he evolved a new system by which he believed he could make it pay. The employer took a different viewpoint and the plan was rejected. Jackling went to other capitalists. They derided him. He persisted. At the end of four years of tireless capital-hunting, he got the start he wanted. Operations began. In a short time the mining world was amazed. Jackling's system not only has made it profitable to operate in light deposits, but has doubled the world's supply of copper.

Keep hammering long enough and hard enough and YOU will get results. That is why I am at you with this again. I'm campaigning for success, yours and mine.

I'll convince you yet that whatever you really determine to have, you get.

WORK and WILL and WIN.

Power

Napoleon Hill

If *success* depends upon power, and if power is *organized effort,* and if the first step in the direction of organization is a *definite purpose,* then one may easily see why such a purpose is essential.

Until a man selects a *definite purpose* in life he dissipates his energies and spreads his thoughts over so many subjects and in so many different directions that they lead not to power, but to indecision and weakness.

With the aid of a small reading glass you can teach yourself a great lesson on the value of *organized effort.* Through the use of such a glass you can focus the sun-rays on a *definite* spot so strongly that they will burn a hole through a plank. Remove the glass (which represents the *definite purpose*) and the same rays of sun may shine on that same plank for a million years without burning it.

A thousand electric dry batteries, when properly organized and connected together with wires, will produce enough power to run a good sized piece of machinery for several hours, but take those same cells singly, disconnected, and not one of them would exert enough energy to turn the machinery over once. The faculties of your mind might properly be likened to those dry cells.

Source: *The Law of Success*. The Ralston University Press, 1928, Vol. II, pp. 44–45.

Contribution

Rich Winograd

It is estimated that today's college graduate will work in five different fields before arriving at a long term career. That's five different fields, not five different jobs. Clearly part of the reason for this is a lack of definiteness of purpose, which is a tremendous negative. Dr. Hill's study of success principles states "that 98 out of every 100 persons stumble through life because they never really define their goals and start toward them with Definiteness of Purpose."

However job change, career change and even location change which are so prevalent today, are not always negative or an indication of lack of Definiteness of Purpose. D.C. Jackling's story demonstrates this. While he may have bounced from teamster to teacher to engineer, he did so as part of a plan, fueled by a burning desire to achieve.

Dr. Hill teaches that "Definiteness of Purpose makes you aware of opportunities related to your major purpose and it inspires the courage to act on them." This is exactly what Jackling's story shows. While he may have changed jobs and careers and even cities, he did not change his goals. Each new venture was simply a new opportunity along the same path. His path may have twisted and turned but the goals never did.

And Jackling acted on those new opportunities, with creative vision, enthusiasm and personal initiative. He also went the extra mile in his endeavors and learned from the adversities he faced. If Definiteness of Purpose is the starting point of all achievement (and it clearly is) then Creative Vision, Enthusiasm, Personal Initiative, Going the Extra Mile and Learning from Adversity and Defeat are all markers on the path beyond the starting point. Jackling possessed them all and he put them all into action, directed towards his goals – towards his definite major purpose.

D.C. Jackling's story is similar to that of Andrew Carnegie's. Jackling started working as a teamster on a farm. Carnegie started working as a laborer in a steel mill. Because of Jackling's unwillingness to settle and his burning desire to seek opportunity and earn more money, he went on to become a successful businessman in the mining industry. Because of Carnegie's unwillingness to settle and his burning desire to produce the highest quality steel possible, he went on to become a business icon as well.

Today's business icons have followed the same path by using the same principles.

Coincidence? Hardly.

Commonality, based on goals, fueled by a burning desire and definiteness of purpose? Absolutely.

The Master "Scoop"

George Harrison Phelps

There is as much difference between planning and doing as there is between winning and losing. Merely to plan is merely to dream, and to dream without transforming your mental visions into living, potential realities, is to hit your own business below the belt.

Follow up your plan with action. The world always respects a man who ACTS because he displays CONTROL OVER CRISES.

Charles H. Grasty was publishing the *Baltimore News* back in 1904 when the big Baltimore fire occurred. His plant, with other millions in business property, was ruined. A cellarful of twisted iron and steel was all that remained of the magnificent institution at 9 p.m.

Long before the flames had eaten away the stalwart walls, Mr. Grasty was on one of the few remaining telephone wires still in operation, arranging to publish temporarily on the premises of the Washington (D.C.) *Post*. And at midnight he was on his way to New York. Immediately on his arrival there he telephoned to Adolph S. Ochs, owner of the plant of the *Philadelphia Times*. The *Times* had been merged with the *Ledger* and the plant was lying idle. The conversation lasted just thirty seconds. As told by Jerome P. Fleishmann it was substantially as follows:

"Hello. Is this Mr. Ochs?"

"Yes. Who is it?"

"Grasty—the *Baltimore News*."

"Where are you?"

"I'm in New York."

"Awfully sorry to hear of your loss."

"Everything has been destroyed in Baltimore. How about the *Philadelphia Times* plant?"

"That plant is at your service."

"What's the price?"

"Go and take it, and if you and I can't agree upon a price later, why we'll leave the matter to a third party."

"Thanks. That's satisfactory. I'll take it."

Ten minutes after this conversation was concluded arrangements had been made to pack and ship the *Times* machinery and accessories to Baltimore, where, while the fire was still raging, Mr. Grasty secured an option on a large building beyond the danger zone.

In two weeks the *News* was being printed in its own temporary quarters. And there, too, were being printed the editions of a morning contemporary that had also been burned out. The *News* did not miss an issue.

Mr. Grasty is the type of man who thinks and acts.

Had he only dreamed and "planned," he would have been listed simply as "one of the many who lost." As it was, his action was the talk of the newspaper world for months. Even today it strikes up a note of admiration among reminiscent editors.

Think of yourself in Mr. Grasty's place. But don't sit and wait for the test of fire. Carry his example into your daily work. Carry it back into those parts of your business that you are ashamed of. We all have them.

FOLLOW UP YOUR PLANS WITH ACTION.

Formula for Initiative and Leadership

Napoleon Hill

Having chosen a *definite chief aim* as my life-work I now understand it to be my duty to transform this purpose into reality.

Therefore, I will form the habit of taking some *definite* action each day that will carry me one step nearer the attainment of my *definite chief aim.*

I know that *procrastination* is a deadly enemy of all who would become leaders in any undertaking, and I will eliminate this habit from my make-up by:

1. Doing some one definite thing each day, that ought to be done, without anyone telling me to do it.
2. Looking around until I find at least one thing that I can do each day, that I have not been in the habit of doing, and that will be of value to others, without expectation of pay.
3. Telling at least one other person, each day, of the value of practicing this habit of doing something that ought to be done without being told to do it.

I can see that the muscles of the body become strong in proportion to the extent to which they are used, therefore I understand that the *habit of initiative* also becomes fixed in proportion to the extent that it is practiced.

I realize that the place to begin developing the *habit of initiative* is in the small, commonplace things connected with my daily work, therefore I will go at my work each day as if I were doing it solely for the purpose of developing this necessary *habit of initiative.*

I understand that by practicing this *habit* of taking the *initiative* in connection with my daily work I will be not only developing that habit, but I will also be attracting the attention of those who will place greater value on my services as a result of this practice.

Source: *The Law of Success.* The Ralston University Press, 1928, Vol. III, pp. 44–45.

Don't Get Scooped

Gregory S. Reid

It's been said that no one has an original idea—they just had that idea before someone else had it. Taking that concept even further, many people have similar, great ideas; yet, it is those who act on them first who get to reap credit and the rewards for them.

In the newspaper industry, this concept is known as "breaking news," and those who delay in bringing their stories to the printed page are the ones who are left shaking their heads, wondering how they got scooped. They had the idea and the information, but they failed to do anything with it.

Our dreams are a visual predictor of what we can accomplish and who we can become. But, if we leave them as dreams which we constantly replay in our heads, they'll never see the light of day. Eventually, we'll stand by as somebody else does what we wanted to do, becomes who we wanted to be, and lives the life we envisioned in our future.

Charles Grasty had a dream, and his dream became the *Baltimore News*. Grasty acted on his dream. But Grasty knew something few people do—he knew that taking action extended beyond the inception of a dream and is often the reason why a business or an idea thrives, instead of dies. Grasty had to take action when the big Baltimore fire ignited his plant. In doing so, he not only saved his publication, but he set his company up for further growth and notoriety. In fact, Gratsy's actions in transplanting his company became "breaking news" in the newspaper business.

Dreams which come to us when we're awake or sleeping are an important part of our future. In fact, they've played a paramount role in many of the greatest inventions and successes in history. Samuel Taylor Coleridge's esteemed poem, "Kubla Kahn," came to him in a dream. A dream gave Elias Howe the answer he needed to invent the sewing machine needle. Both of them immediately acted upon their dreams, penning their legacy or inventing it. Without their actions, their dreams would have had no purpose.

News isn't news until it's reported. Your ideas and plans will never become a reality until you take that first step to make it happen. Every delay on your part is an opportunity to someone else.

If you've got a dream, an idea, or a goal, you'll need a plan. But we could all learn a valuable lesson from Grasty and the newspaper business. Leaving a plan idle and failing to take action on it is a surefire way to make sure that it becomes yesterday's news. The competition is just waiting to scoop your dreams. After all, you're not the only person with a great idea. But you can be the first person to do something about it. And that is exactly what breaking news is all about.

The Lamp-Lighter

George Harrison Phelps

Better the little things that you are doing and the big things will take care of themselves. The little, almost insignificant details are often the vital ones. Just as a grain of musk will scent a room for twenty years, so may your carelessness in seemingly trivial matters affect your business and personal success. The mixing of mortar for the foundation of a twenty-story building is an insignificant detail as compared to the great engineering problems that go into its construction. Mix your mortar well or when the storms break your business structure will sway and crumble about your head.

Set an example for those who follow you—teach them the value of the little things you do. Not long ago on the rolling downs of an English camp, Harry Lauder told a story of the Lamp-Lighter to ten thousand soldiers just before they entered the first-line trenches.

"One evening, in the gloaming of a northern town, I was sitting in my parlor window when I saw an old man with a pole on his shoulder come along," said Lauder. "He was a lamp-lighter and made the lamp opposite my window dance into brightness. Interested in his work, I watched him pass along until the gloaming gathered around and I could see him no more. However, I knew just where he was, for other lamps flashed into flame. Having completed his task, he disappeared into a side street.

Those lights burned on through the night, making it bright and safe for those who should come behind him. An avenue of lights through the traffic and dangers of the darkness. Boys," cried Lauder, "think of that man who lit the lamp!"

What he was doing was a little thing—just the simple lighting of a few old street lamps. Night after night—unfailingly the same route—the same lamps.

You are doing the same thing in a grander and nobler way. By doing well the little things, you are lighting the avenues of your business—that will make it safe when things are dark and storms come.

Watch the little things!

A Code of Ethics

Napoleon Hill

"I wish to be of service to my fellow men as I journey through life. To do this I have adopted this creed as a guide to be followed in dealing with my fellow-beings:

"To train myself so that never, under any circumstances, will I find fault with any person, no matter how much I may disagree with him or how inferior his work may be, as long as I know he is sincerely trying to do his best.

"To respect my country, my profession and myself. To be honest and fair with my fellow men, as I expect them to be honest and fair with me. To be a loyal citizen of my country. To speak of it with praise, and act always as a worthy custodian of its good name. To be a person whose name carries weight wherever it goes.

"To base my expectations of reward on a solid foundation of service rendered. To be willing to pay the price of success in honest effort. To look upon my work as an opportunity to be seized with joy and made the most of, and not as a painful drudgery to be reluctantly endured.

"To remember that success lies within myself—in my own brain. To expect difficulties and to force my way through them.

"To avoid procrastination in all its forms, and never, under any circumstances, put off until tomorrow any duty that should be performed today.

"Finally, to take a good grip on the joys of life, so I may be courteous to men, faithful to friends, true to God—a fragrance in the path I tread."

Source: *The Law of Success.* The Ralston University Press, 1928, Vol. V, pp. 45, 47.

Confessions of a Neat Freak: The Habit of Self-Discipline

Christopher Lake

I was at Starbuck's this morning and while waiting for my triple venti latte I saw a wayward straw wrapper on the floor. Almost automatically I bent down and put the paper in the trashcan.

"Thank you," came a voice behind me. I turned, expecting to see a barista, and was surprised to find a smiling customer in a sport coat and tie. "It seems like I'm always picking up trash somewhere. Thanks for doing that," he repeated.

What could be more insignificant than a paper wrapper? How little effort does it take to pick up litter? I could have noticed the wrapper and told myself that someone else would pick it up—after all, there are employees in the coffeeshop who get paid for that sort of thing. And nobody could be injured or affected in any way by a little piece of paper.

Or am I wrong?

Obviously my casual attention to detail meant something to my litter-conscious friend, enough to elicit a comment and brighten his day, if only for a moment. In return, I was rewarded by his response and came to the office with a smile on my face. Did anyone else in the shop see our exchange? What sort of "positive energy" was felt by the people around us?

Some people might call me fastidious; truly I am fussy about neatness, and it's my second nature to clean up little things like straw wrappers and spilled cream and sugar. My habits are the outward signs of an ingrained sense of self-discipline. Noticing details is relatively easy; taking a moment to address those details requires the self-discipline and presence of mind to act, not make excuses.

Dr. Hill defines the principle of Self-Discipline as "taking possession of your own mind." I often describe self-discipline as an extension of Definiteness of Purpose: knowing what you want and intend to achieve leads to applying self-discipline to achieve your goals. Important details quickly become apparent as you work toward achieving your definite major purpose, and you are motivated to act promptly.

The story of the lamplighter illustrates the value of a careful, disciplined approach to life. Countless persons benefited from the lamplighter's work and his absence would be sorely missed. Are you working with a purpose or just showing up? Where can you see some lingering details in your own business? Have you made follow-up phone calls, returned voicemail messages, and replied to important e-mails? Whose success depends on you?

Like every skill, self-discipline grows through practice. Take a few minutes to attend to the small, maybe insignificant details you come across. Don't just make an excuse that you're too busy or it's not that important. Pick up the litter, or offer a helping hand. You'll soon find that action becomes your automatic response to life. Imagine the increase in your productivity and effectiveness. Imagine the reduction in stress. Paradoxically, the habit of self-discipline leads to a greater sense of freedom and satisfaction. Go ahead — get started right now.

Guynemier

George Harrison Phelps

Did you ever notice how frequently our troubles dissolve in the light of other tasks—how good hard work and complete absorption will drive away our worries and our ills? Many a man has caught his balance on the brink of some disaster just because something distracted his attention. It is dangerous to be too well acquainted with your own troubles. They will absorb all of your thought, if you let them. It is almost a statutory offense for a man to be anything but an optimist these days. That isn't enough, however—be a working optimist. Grab some big idea in your business, in your home, anywhere, feed it every ounce of thought and energy you have—and then watch those troubles leave you for other soil more fertile.

When the great European war broke out, Georges Guynemier was ill. In fact, he believed that he could live but a short time longer. Tuberculosis, the doctor had told him—and he knew from the racking cough and twinging pain that it must be true. Yet he was a patriot and he determined to be of some service to his country before he died. He attempted to enlist. The examining physicians shook their heads sadly and bade him go back home. He could never stand the rigors of military life, they said.

Guynemier went home as directed. But the next day he was back again, in another recruiting office. Again he was sent away. Twice more he tried and twice more met stern rejection.

But he persisted. The fifth time he was permitted to enlist for light duties in the aviation section. It was but a few days before his mechanical skill attracted the attention of officers, and he was made a mechanician. It was his chance—and no chance went past him unheeded.

So thorough and so skillful and so persistent was this young man of 23, a few months before half dead from tuberculosis, that he won the rank of pilot, his goal. From this day the story of "King of the Aces Guynemier" is no longer an obscure page in the annals of the war. The name rings throughout the world. All France reveres it. It is the name of the most brilliant and most daring hero of the air that the war has produced.

The winged devils of the German army dreaded him. Sixty-four of their planes staggered in the clouds and dropped under his seemingly infallible machine gun fire. Little wonder the women of France put their babies to bed with the consoling assurance that "the Germans can't harm us tonight; Captain Guynemier is near."

The frail tubercular boy of 23, first an "Ace," then "King of the Aces," was the idol of his nation. And finally when he soared out into the air and never returned, there was grief and mourning as heartfelt and sincere as though every mother in France had lost a son.

And—what about young Guynemier, if he had been no more than an optimist? Why, he would have gone home after the first examination, reconciled himself to the thought that he had failed—and gone off somewhere and died.

And that would have ended the story of Guynemier. But it also happened that this young man was a WORKING optimist.

He wrapped himself around a bigger thing than his troubles and became the hero of two continents.

BE A WORKING OPTIMIST.

Service

Napoleon Hill

If you serve an ungrateful master, serve him the more. Put God in your debt. Every stroke shall be repaid. The longer the payment is withholden, the better for you; for compound interest on compound interest is the rate and usage in this exchequer. –Emerson

Out of resistance comes strength, therefore render the best service of which you are capable, regardless of the monetary compensation you are receiving for your efforts.

What you want is power, and this comes by organizing and exercising all of your faculties to the limit, just as an arm grows strong out of constant use.

Never mind about the pay. Take a lesson from the farmer who plows his ground, fertilizes it, plants the seed and then waits for the reaction which is sure to provide him with a rich harvest.

Plant the seed of service that is right in quality and quantity, then watch what happens when you have established the reputation of being a person who always renders better service than that which is paid for.

If you will form the habit of rendering more service and better service than that which you contract to perform, very soon the law of increasing returns will begin to work in your favor, you will profit by contrast, and your harvest time will have come, for you will be eagerly sought and willingly paid for more than you actually do.

The cheat, the defaulter, the gambler cannot extort the benefit, cannot extort the knowledge of material

and moral nature which his honest care and pains
yield to the operative. The law of nature is,
do the thing and you shall have the power.

Source: *Napoleon Hill's Magazine*. July, 1921, p. 21.

The Magic Key

George Harrison Phelps

A successful man is always interesting. Everything about him is interesting. His valet could go on the lecture platform and make a fortune. The public would flock to hear him. His most trivial anecdote would be attended with bated breath.

For we are interested in success. We are more interested in success than in anything else in the world. And when we hear of a man who has attained it, we rush up to him with curious eyes. A bit of star dust has fallen among us. We would study it and know more of the Heavens.

Instinctively we compare him with ourselves. We are curious to see what he has that we have not. We are a little envious, perhaps. A little disparaging. But we are intensely curious.

And so we are often pleased to discover that he is very ordinary, after all. Very like ourselves. No stronger, no handsomer, no better trained, no more industrious, no smarter. We are rather mystified. It seems like a trick of fate—his success. An accident.

But, it never is.

He merely has a quality we overlooked, without which brain and brawn and labor never scale the peaks. No, not genius. Something we don't have to be born with, thank God. Call it what you will. The quality of doing something no one else has thought to do—and doing it without being told. Call it creative action. Call it INITIATIVE.

The Prince of Wales once visited Pittsburg. When his private car drew into the smoky yards, there were manly railroad and steel men waiting to see the future king. But there was only one who used his initiative. He was an obscure superintendent of the Pennsylvania Lines. He was twenty-five years old, and his name was Andy Carnegie.

As the Prince alighted, Carnegie sprang forward and offered the titled stranger an exciting ride on a locomotive. As the two young men—one a prince by virtue of his birth, and the other by virtue of his competency—clung to the narrow seat of the engineer's cab and were jolted along the crooked track, there began the springtime of a friendship which in its autumn brought much business to the Pittsburgh steel mills.

And so here is the magic key that opens the doors of gold. Each one of us wears it around his neck. And yet we stand outside helplessly and cry to get in.

Tear the key loose! Throw open the doors!

Use your INITIATIVE.

Salesmanship

Napoleon Hill

In the field of salesmanship it is a well-known fact that no salesman is successful in selling others until he has first made a good job of selling *himself.* Stated conversely, no salesman can do his best to sell others without sooner or later selling himself that which he is trying to sell to others.

Any statement that a person repeats over and over again for the purpose of inducing others to believe it, he, also, will come to believe, and this holds good whether the statement is false or true.

You can now see the advantage of making it your business to *talk initiative, think initiative, eat initiative, sleep initiative* and *practice initiative*. By so doing you are becoming a person of *initiative* and *leadership*, for it is a well-known fact that people will readily, willingly and voluntarily follow the person who shows by his actions that he is a person of *initiative*.

Source: *The Law of Success*. The Ralston University Press, 1928, Vol. III, p. 85.

Roosevelt

George Harrison Phelps

We are raising potatoes in the back yard. Radishes are doing well in the hanging baskets. The old mine has been reopened, and they are trailing the ore deeper into the heart of the hills. At night, the sluice gates are drawn up and refreshing floods of mountain rain stream out over the transformed deserts.

We didn't do all this ten or twenty years ago. Few of us thought it necessary to cultivate intensively a virgin world. And anyway, the obstacles were too great, it seemed. So the surface mine was exploited and abandoned; and the great dry plains were left to the hunter and his prey.

It was only when men of vision saw new wealth in the old coffers, that we began to retrace our steps, with open eyes.

Back in 1884 the intrepid "Teddy" went out West in search of health and big game. Up in the "bad lands" of North Dakota he found the antlers of two great elks still locked in the death struggle. Here he built himself a log cabin and went into the business of hunting. But there was no great profit in hunting, and noticing the excellent condition of the game he encountered, the thought occurred to him that cattle, too, ought to thrive there, and he decided to try out his theory.

His intention got noised about the neighborhood and the good advice began to come in.

"You can't raise cattle up here, sir," was the warning of an old ranchman; "it's too wild, and the seasons are too severe. It's never been done."

"Well, it's going to be done!" replied Roosevelt, and he immediately drove several thousand head up from Texas and Arkansas.

The story of the three years that followed, with blizzards to weather, and prairie fires, and "bad men," and cattle thieves to fight, reads like romance. The neighborhood theory was not to be disproved without a struggle. Hardships there were, and dangers. By round-up time the maltese-branded herds would be scattered over hundreds of miles of unfenced prairie, and once it was necessary to spend thirty-six hours in the saddle to save them from destruction. But they were saved, and they grew fat, and "Elkhorn Ranch" on the Little Missouri prospered.

A pioneer with vision once looked beyond what had been done, and saw what might be done—then did it.

And experience is teaching us all what the Colonel taught Dakota Territory way back in the Eighties—that half our resources have lain untouched because we lacked the vision and the energy to develop them.

Don't let this be true of you as a merchant or a salesman. Don't overlook any of the profit your territory holds for you. Pay no attention to the calamity howlers. They will "get you" if you do.

Achievement is Born of Sacrifice

Napoleon Hill

There can be no great achievement without a corresponding sacrifice. Christ gave his life that his philosophy might be planted in the human heart forever.

Think of one person, if you can, who has risen to fame or rendered the world a lasting service without sacrifice. Usually the value of the service rendered is in proportion to the sacrifice out of which it sprung.

Nature does not appear to favor the perpetuation of ideas or ideals which are not born of sacrifice and nurtured amid hardship and struggle. From the lowest mineral substance to the highest form of animal organism Nature gives evidence aplenty of Her favoritism for that which is born of hardship, resistance and struggle.

The hardiest and finest trees of the forest are those which grew slowly and overcame the greatest resistance. No hot-house vegetable can equal those that are grown in the open, in opposition to the elements of the weather.

In a practical, material world of business, finance and industry we see evidence on every hand of the soundness of this philosophy. Successes that are achieved overnight seldom endure. The greatest achievements in business are those which began at the very bottom, were based upon sound fundamentals and experienced seemingly impossible sacrifice. Before we envy Henry Ford his success we should meditate upon the struggles and hardships which he survived before he created the first Ford automobile. All of us would enjoy his great wealth but few of us would be willing to pay for it in sacrifice, as he has done.

If you are taking your baptism of fire and paying the price of sacrifice with faith in your handiwork, no matter what station in life you are striving to achieve you are apt to realize it if you carry on without losing faith, without turning back, without losing confidence in yourself and in the fundamental principle which insures achievement that corresponds to the nature and extent of your sacrifice.

Source: *Napoleon Hill's Magazine*. February, 1922, inside back cover.

Roosevelt: Vision and Applied Faith

Eliezer A. Alperstein

With the aid of radar, pilots are now able to fly through thick fog and land their planes safely even though they can't see the ground below. Radar beams, which can't be seen or felt, guide them to the runway where they set their planes down as if they were flying through clear, blue skies.

A pilot has to know where he is going and has to have the skills and knowledge to pilot his plane to the destination he has chosen, yet there will also be those radar beams which can't be seen or felt which will guide him along the way.

I think it would be safe to say that our lives are much the same. We need to know where we are going and envision ourselves successfully landing at our chosen destination in life. Yet there is an intangible factor which will lead to our success which can be called many names: luck, chance, fate, or destiny.

Dr. Hill described this intangible as "Applied Faith." According to his philosophy, Infinite Intelligence will guide us on our way through a series of hunches, ideas, and events unfolding with synchronicity. This process appears to be random and chaotic, yet it is often the magic ingredient which places someone at the right place at the right time after he has done all of the preparation and hard work which was humanly possible.

Roosevelt was one of America's greatest presidents. He was known for his bravery, vision, and "can do" attitude. It appeared as if he could simply "will" things into being. The same could be said for Lincoln or Reagan who made it their goals to preserve the union and defeat communism respectively.

The principle of Applied Faith is the connecting factor between the physical world and the spiritual world, between the will of the individual and the Divine Will. It is what makes the seemingly impossible possible, the "it can't be done" to "I've done it."

A person needs vision and energy to pursue his goals. Yet most successful people will also admit that there was an added ingredient to their success which helped push them to the top which was beyond their control.

Our visions may take us to places where the fog is thick, where there are blizzards, prairie fires, thieves to fight, and where we may have to stay in the saddle for thirty-six hours in order to save our dreams from destruction, yet with a little "luck," we'll be able to follow those silent and invisible beams which will guide us on our way until we reach our chosen destination.

Helping America

George Harrison Phelps

You want to be a good American, don't you? In fact, if I should intimate even slightly that you were not a good American, you would doubtless fly in a rage and retaliate upon me with countless examples of your patriotism.

You did all that was asked of you.

You gave freely of your substance. You wore the emblem of Liberty upon your coat.

Perhaps you bade farewell to some loved one as he marched away to give his life, if need be, that your country might endure.

A service flag flew proudly at your window, and the neighbors bowed to it with reverence as they passed your door.

Your table boasted few luxuries, and the spade had turned your lawn to rows of garden stuff.

Your wrath was sometimes uncontrollable as you talked to your friends about the things our enemy was doing.

Yes—You're a good American.

But what about the gossip that you hear? Do you let it pass you by? Or do you clutch at each insinuation and rail at all the little things you fail to understand?

Do you stop to think that our men in public life are only human, and do you forget their faults in the light of bigger things?

Do you give them your encouragement? or do you criticize, and sneer, and SPREAD those thoughts to make their way the harder?

Perhaps some of you remember when our own Lincoln was being criticized in '64. His answer might well be studied now. "Gentlemen," he said, "suppose that all the property you were worth was in gold, and you put it in the hands of Blondin, the famous tight-rope walker, to carry across Niagara on a rope. Would you shake the rope while he was passing over it, or keep shouting to him, 'Blondin, stoop a little more; go a little faster?'

"No, I'm sure you would not. You would hold your breath, as well as your tongue, and keep your hands off until he was safely over."

Now, if ever, is the time when we should keep our hands about us and show the kind of stuff our patriotism is made of.

LET'S HELP INSTEAD OF HINDER.

The Dreamers

Napoleon Hill

Cherish your visions; cherish your ideals;
cherish the music that stirs in your heart;
the beauty that forms in your mind;
the loveliness that drapes your purest thoughts,
for out of them will grow all delightful
conditions, all heavenly environment;
of these, if you but remain true to them,
your world will at last be built.

Civilization owes its existence to the dreamers of the past. Civilization cannot advance ahead of its idealists and dreamers.

They are the pattern makers of the race. The seething masses have always followed the paths which the dreamers have hewn.

Now the dreamers are about to take the glory out of conquest and war. Woodrow Wilson sacrificed himself as a target when he made the first step in stripping conquerors of their glory. Soon other dreamers will dare to follow the trail he has opened and war will then be a disgrace and those who advocate or engage in it will be social outcasts and brigands.

Even the individual who cherishes a lofty ideal in his heart is apt to realize it. Columbus dreamed of another world and discovered it. Copernicus dreamed of a multiplicity of worlds and revealed them. Cherish your visions and your dreams for they are the blue-prints of your ultimate attainment.

Your dreams can carry you to any station in life you cherish. If you are unworthy of the position you seek remember that your aspirations and your dreams, operating through the law of auto-suggestion, can rebuild your character and make you worthy.

The White House is none too high as a mark of attainment for which to strive. Include it in your dreams and you have already taken the first step toward realization.

In all human affairs there are efforts, and there are results, and the strength of the effort is the measure of the result. Chance is not. "Gifts," powers, material, intellectual and spiritual possessions are the fruits of effort; they are thoughts completed, objects accomplished, visions realized.

Source: *Napoleon Hill's Magazine*. July, 1921, p. 25.

The Butcher

George Harrison Phelps

The other day I happened to meet a friend who publishes one of our best automobile trade papers. He is a big man in the publishing world—and his bigness is usually displayed in his constant desire to "help-a-long." Hardly a day goes by but he manages to give some deserving chap a boost to bigger things and greater opportunities.

He is happiest when he is doing little things for these friends of his—and his address book includes many a country salesman, and general managers by the dozen.

So can you wonder that this man has a devoted following that believe in his preachments as did the ancient Greeks in the Delphian Oracle?

He isn't Delphic, but he does stay astraddle.

Like a true son of Erin, he sails in with his shillalah when blows are needed.

He is no respecter of position unless that position has been won thru sheer merit—won in the rendering of service for better work.

"Frank," I said, "why don't you take a page in that magazine of yours and tell the dealers and salesmen to be careful that they don't miss the handwriting on the wall. The big difficulty," I told him, "is the natural dislike that the average salesman has for breaking into new fields, his aversion to developing a commercial business, perhaps, during these times when passenger car production is restricted and sales of commercial vehicles are necessary if his employer's business is to go on."

"I'll gladly do as you suggest," he said, "but in the meantime why don't YOU tell YOUR boys the fable of 'The Ox and the Ass?'

"The Ox, it seems, was just a little bit inclined to be lazy—he didn't like those war times when everybody had to carry on the work of the boys who had gone—when the farmer was hustling at top-notch speed to harvest a bumper crop. He preferred the old days when things came easy, and he could munch his cud beneath the shade of a friendly tree, with none but the kind of work he was used to and liked to do the best.

"One sultry day, when the farmer had been a bit impatient because the Ox had loafed, this Ox said to the Ass, 'I'm going to quit. You can work your head off if you want to, but I'm going to take things easy for a while.' And so the Ox laid off and went back to his old habits, and the shady tree and his cud.

"After a few days his conscience pricked him, I suppose, and he said to the Ass, 'Say, old man, did the farmer say anything about me today?' 'Not a word,' said the Ass, 'he didn't even seem to know you weren't on the job.' The next day the Ox asked the same question and received the same answer.

"After a time the Ox began to feel guilty again, and once more he said to the Ass, 'Did the farmer say anything about me today?' 'No,' said the Ass, 'not a word; he didn't seem to know you weren't on the job. But wait, I forgot to tell you—I did see him stop at the Slaughter House on his way home and have a long talk with the butcher.'"

A Good Joke

Napoleon Hill

Here's a good joke to play on your employer: Get to your work a little earlier and leave a little later than you are supposed to. Handle his tools as if they belonged to you. Go out of your way to say a kind word about him to your fellow workers. When there is extra work that needs to be done, volunteer to do it. Do not show surprise when he "gets on to you" and offers you the head of the department or a partnership in the business, for this is the best part of the "joke."

Source: *The Law of Success.* The Ralston University Press, 1928, Vol. VII, p. 104.

"As He Thinketh"

George Harrison Phelps

Be a neighbor—not a knocker. So long as men come together in business, in the home, in the church—in fact, while human habitation covers the globe, the man devout in the Religion of Neighborliness, who touches with surest hand the greatest number of human hearts, will be a giant among his fellows.

There is an old story on this point that I want to tell you—an old story of a Quaker and his quaint philosophy.

He stood one day watering his horse at the village trough when a new neighbor paused with not over-pleasant greeting.

"What manner of people live in the village?" the new-coming resident asked.

"What manner of people didst thee live amongst before?" retorted the amicable old Quaker, affectionately patting the neck of his horse.

"The people in the town I came from," answered the stranger, "were mean. They were narrow, they were forever suspicious, and quick to take unfair advantage."

"Then," said the Quaker, "I am sorry, for thee will find the same manner of people here."

And the newcomer found it as the old Quaker had told him.

Again the Quaker chanced to be at the trough when another stranger came into the village. He, too, inquired about the temper of the populace, and to him as well the Quaker put the question, "What manner of people didst thee live amongst before?"

A broad and cordial smile overspread the features of the stranger as he spoke. "Friend," he said, "there are none finer than the people I left behind. They were neighbors and I loved them. It was hard for me to leave—I loved them all, but I had to journey on."

The face of the old Quaker beamed with welcome. "Be of good cheer, my neighbor," he said, "for thee will find the same fine people here."

And again it was as the old Quaker said.

"As he thinketh in his heart, so is he."

It is an old proverb, fraught with meaning and with wisdom. It is not a vague platitude; neither is it a myth of sentiment. It is a fundamental law of life, as sure and true in its working as the law that gives the sun its heat.

And so I say to you, fellow business men and salesmen:

Tell me a little about YOUR town and YOUR neighbors and I'll tell you a lot about YOU and YOUR business.

Every Thought You Release

Napoleon Hill

If all your acts toward others, and even your thoughts of others, are registered in your sub-conscious mind, through the principle of Auto-suggestion, thereby building your own character in exact duplicate of your *thoughts* and *acts*, can you not see how important it is to guard those acts and thoughts?

Stated in another way, every *act* and every *thought* you release modifies your own character in exact conformity with the nature of the act or thought, and your character is a sort of center of magnetic attraction which attracts to you the people and conditions that harmonize with it.

You cannot indulge in an act toward another person without having first created the nature of that act in your own *thought*, and *you cannot release a thought without planting the sum and substance and nature of it in your own sub-conscious mind, there to become a part and parcel of your own character.*

Grasp this simple principle and you will understand why you cannot afford to hate or envy another person. You will also understand why you cannot afford to strike back, in kind, at those who do you an injustice. Likewise, you will understand the injunction, "Return good for evil."

Source: *Think and Grow Rich.* The Ralston Society, 1937, p. 229.

The Song of the Robin

George Harrison Phelps

It is a wonderful thing today to talk with men who are cheerful and optimistic and determined. We talk to lots of men like that here at the Works.

They are an inspiration and they are doing their bit, too—and doing it mightily—for cheerfulness and optimism and determination are creative things. They are never destructive.

They are the qualities that pay big dividends—for they are the solution in which most troubles are dissolved.

A cheerful man is welcome everywhere.

He has a product that is always in demand and by the measure of his cheerfulness he prospers.

This is no time for gloom, or fear, or pessimism.

It is time for us to show the indomitable spirit of our race—to smile—and sing and fight.

Perhaps Charles R. Trowbridge's story of the wounded robin will help a bit. Let me tell it to you.

"The other day," said Trowbridge, "I ran across a robin with one leg broken off. I said to myself, 'What a pity; what little else is there left for him to live for now—hobbling around on one leg?'

"And then what do you think that injured robin did? Other birds were singing their evenings songs and he joined in. There was no note that differed from the song that the robin with two legs sings; there was no indication in the music that came from the little throat that it was grieving over the loss of the leg.

"And I thought, if this robin can disdain such a disaster and rise so far above as to sing undismayed and without a change of tone, how much more ought man, the summit of animal creation, cast aside his troubles, his worries, his failures, and get cheerfulness in his soul.

"Cheerfulness will do much to make the way easier—easier for you and easier for others."

And so if things look bleak, and you feel discouraged, just think of the robin with the lost leg, singing its evening song.

Has It Ever Occurred to You?

Napoleon Hill

Has it ever occurred to you that every failure and every mistake from which you survive and every obstacle which you master, develops in you wisdom, strategy and self-mastery, without which you could accomplish no great undertaking?

No man likes to meet with failure, yet every failure can be turned into a stepping stone that will carry one to the heights of achievement, if the lessons taught by the failure are organized, classified and used as a guide.

If your failures embitter you toward your fellowmen and develop cynicism in your heart they will soon destroy your usefulness; but, if you accept them as necessary teachers and build them into a shield, you can make of them an impenetrable protection.

Vanity prompts us to give more thought to our triumphs than we do to our failures, yet, if we profit by the experience of those who have accomplished most in the world, we will see that a man never needs to watch himself so closely as when he begins to attain success, because success often causes a slackening of effort and a letting down of that eternal vigilance which causes a man to throw the power of his combative nature into that which he is doing.

Source: *Napoleon Hill's Magazine.* February, 1922, back cover.

Be of Good Cheer

Cheri Lutton

When I think about the robin's song and story, I hear the sounds of the robin's cheerfulness in my mind's ear. Dr. Napoleon Hill knew all too well how vital a positive mental attitude plays in the development of a successful leader. The robin knew about the power of enthusiasm as a natural instinct, perhaps feeling that the only option in life is to be happy!

I believe that many of Napoleon Hill's principles of success revolve around the wisdom that "cheerfulness will do much to make the way easier for you and easier for others." I know that in my personal and professional experiences, the joy of life is what moves me from moment to moment. The simple experience of being alive can be an awesome and extraordinary event that transforms and uplifts one's spirit.

Whenever I run on my favorite trail, I enjoy this feeling in partnership with My Creator. I ponder on the goodness that is within the core of our universe, and how Infinite Intelligence, as coined by Dr. Hill, has majestically provided for each and every one of us. That state of cheerfulness blended with gratitude, my friend, can begin an endless spiral of joy that evolves into rapture without bounds.

Let's explore a few of the other principles, such as going the extra mile, a pleasing personality, personal initiative, a positive mental attitude, enthusiasm, and maintenance of sound health.

Think about how closely each of these principles are linked to cheerfulness. Going the extra mile and taking personal initiative will nudge your desire to serve others, and bring about a spirit of helpfulness which will spur your ability to connect with the world and make others cheerful. When you inspire cheerfulness in others, that same quality will reflect itself in you in immeasurable quantities.

A pleasing personality will attract others, including all living creatures, to you, and bring about a sense of joy and fulfillment into your daily experience. Along those lines, a positive mental attitude and enthusiasm will bring your song of joy alive and radiate your day with just the right light to shine throughout your day's journey. Maintenance of sound health will bring to bear all that is needed for you to move along on your path of success, whistling while you work.

Go now and create your medley of good cheer in all that you do and become. Dr. Hill studied this work intensively and discovered these principles to be pivotal in the success of a leader. Each leader he researched has reverberated Hill's words of wisdom, emphasizing the importance of cheerfulness to one's happiness and contribution to the world. A smile, a good deed, a well wish … all make up the stuff of fairy tales that transform the mundane into the miraculous. You can make it all happen!

Reserve Energy

George Harrison Phelps

Neurologists tell us we use a very small part of our mental power. Possibly thirty or forty percent. The same thing is true of our bodies say the doctors, and of our wills say the psychologists, and of our imaginations adds the poet. And certainly of our opportunities thunders the successful man of affairs. Oddly enough they all speak true.

We are everywhere confronted with that mysterious power known as reserve energy.

Every runner knows what it is to get his second wind.

It was reserve energy that dragged the prospector from Death Valley after thirty days without food.

It is reserve energy that makes each one of us a potential success.

Our greatness lies within ourselves.

Fate plays no part in this present-day creed of the business man.

We are artisans of our own destiny. And we become more fearlessly active as we realize our strength. Less willing to recognize the impossible. More scornful of obstacles that stand between ourselves and the Golden Fleece.

Nor is it necessary to ransack Wall Street or Oklahoma or the far seas to illustrate this good American quality.

The winter of 1918 was the most severe that Michigan had experienced in over forty years. Railroads were paralyzed and almost every available freight car was being used by the

Government to transport our troops. Dealers had to have motor cars if they were to stay in business. There was only one way. The cars must be driven over the road. From all corners of the country these dealers came and braved the ice and snow. Sometimes they were stalled in drifts for days and yet on they came — more drivers — more cars — a steady stream for weeks.

Morning after morning, a little ticker up in the telegraph office clicked off its dots and dashes. And then the boy came down and laid a bundle of yellow romances on my desk. They were messages from dealers who were journeying home with cars. And each one told its own particular tale of perseverance and adventure; of ingenuity and courage and triumph.

For the Road has always demanded these qualities of its wayfarers.

Swarthy Bedouins made dangerous the ancient trails of the desert. Cossack renegades haunted the frozen steppes, adding terror to the hardships of ice and snow. Brigands, carabinetti, highwaymen, bandits and apaches used to join the rocks and floods and snow to persecute him who would brave the terrors of the trail. That stirring old ballad, "Boot, saddle, to horse, and away!" was always half cavalier-song and half battle-cry.

Today the ways are less hazardous. The lance and the bludgeon have gone with the years. But often the road still passed over stony hills. The snows still blew and drifted. And so those little messages told of adventures triumphant. Of problems met and solved.

We were proud of those boys who drove our cars away. They caught the spirit of the times. They transported the product of one of the world's largest motor car factories under conditions that seemed impossible. A wonderful thing this reserve energy. It pays to cultivate it.

No Substitute

Napoleon Hill

Those who have cultivated the HABIT of persistence seem to enjoy insurance against failure. No matter how many times they are defeated, they finally arrive up toward the top of the ladder. Sometimes it appears that there is a hidden Guide whose duty is to test men through all sorts of discouraging experiences. Those who pick themselves up after defeat and keep on trying, arrive; and the world cries, "Bravo! I knew you could do it!" The hidden Guide lets no one enjoy great achievement without passing the PERSISTENCE TEST. Those who can't take it, simply do not make the grade.

Source: *Think and Grow Rich*. The Ralston Society, 1937, p. 229.

Lord Nelson

George Harrison Phelps

Before one of the greatest battles of his career, Lord Nelson gave this command: "In case signals cannot be seen or clearly understood, no captain can do wrong if he places his ship alongside that of the enemy."

Nelson had the key to successful salesmanship.

If you get nothing else from these signal messages, set here to help you to greater command, to greater business, to the winning of a full and successful life, get this:

Go every day to the front of the firing line, fully equipped and confident that you are going to sweep the field.

Get close to every prospect. Fire him with your enthusiasm. Make him feel that your proposition will supply his needs completely. Make him feel that your personality, your methods of business, your high standing and the great backing behind you are assurance of the service and satisfaction it is his right to demand.

The spirit of Lord Nelson's command—"no captain can do wrong if he places his ship alongside that of the enemy"—is the spirit of my message to you. To follow it is to prove that you know no fear in the battle of business; that you welcome an encounter hand to hand; that a wide range and a long-distance bombardment is to you a droll monotony.

Go alongside! Go alongside until the powder blisters the paint of the enemy's ships. Get into the prospect's lines of defense. Storm them! Make them your lines of action. Get close. Watch the signals. Fire YOUR BROADSIDE FIRST.

How much greater the thrill, how much quicker the goal is attained by this alert style of attack than by the waiting, vacillating brand of salesmanship. How much more the prospect appreciates the frank, forceful logic of the aggressive salesman than the weak, hesitant plea of the one who lags and is afraid.

Meet them face to face! Go alongside—and board them when you can. A fair and honorable victor is always an object of admiration, even to the vanquished themselves. The closer and harder the battle, the quicker and more glorious the triumph.

Assemble, then, your munitions of fact and reason and argument and get out—now—on the line of battle.

And remember that the man who fights most and fights hardest is the man who wins!

We Win or We Perish!

Napoleon Hill

A long while ago, a great warrior faced a situation which made it necessary for him to make a decision which insured his success on the battlefield. He was about to send his armies against a powerful foe, whose men outnumbered his own. He loaded his soldiers into boats, sailed to the enemy's country, unloaded soldiers and equipment, then gave the order to burn the ships that had carried them. Addressing his men before the first battle, he said, "You see the boats going up in smoke. That means we cannot leave these shores alive unless we win! We now have no choice—we win—or we perish!" They won.

Source: *Think and Grow Rich*. The Ralston Society, 1937, p. 40.

The Motor Transport

George Harrison Phelps

How often you heard a friend or pal say, "If I'm going into this scrap, I want to GET IN IT. I want to see the real show, in France, not here at home, and I want to get there quickly, too!" Of course he did—so did any real red-blooded American with the right stuff in him. I had a chap tell me that the Motor Transport Corps was too tame, that it didn't produce enough action. He seemed to feel that it offered little opportunity for one to mix up in the thick of it; but just listen to this conversation between an officer and a newspaper correspondent:

"You don't hear so much about these motor transport drivers," said the captain, "but don't forget they are part of the big job, and a big part. And don't forget they have dangerous work to do.

"The supplies have got to go forward, whatever the conditions, and I have never yet had a man show any inclination to shrink or dodge or complain when he had to go under heavy fire and deliver his supplies.

"I'll give you an example of their spirit. After a recent hard push we had an afternoon off, so the men arranged a ball game just back of the front with a rival outfit. They had played about two innings when this kid here (pointing to a young driver standing by) came up to bat. Then the fun started.

"Two big German shells lit in the outfield. The rival pitcher turned around to see what the trouble was. Another shell fell just back of second base. Once more the pitcher half-way turned, when the kid at bat called out; 'Aw, what the hell; come on and stick it over.' The pitcher stuck one over and the kid cracked out a double to right.

"Easy work? Would you care to count the machine gun and the bullet holes in this ambulance?"

The count was made and the result showed exactly 73 through various parts of the big frame.

"That's the way it goes," said the captain. "Seventy-three through this one, and many others about the same. But with the work done, when you'd think they were all in after 36 or 48 hours of almost endless going, give 'em a ball game and they've still got nerve enough to forget a volley of German shells with 'Stick it over, kid; stick it over.'"

Degree of Power

Napoleon Hill

The degree of power created by the co-operative effort of any group of people is measured, always, by the nature of the motive which the group is laboring to attain. This may be profitably borne in mind by all who organize group effort for any purpose whatsoever. Find a motive around which men may be induced to rally in a highly emotionalized, enthusiastic spirit of perfect harmony and you have found the starting point for the creation of a Master Mind.

Source: *The Law of Success*. The Ralston University Press, 1928, Vol. VII, pp. 130–131.

The Motor Transport: Teamwork and Enthusiasm

Jim Rohrbach

How far we have come since the Motor Transport Corps. It would be inconceivable today to fight a war without the well-coordinated activities of a variety of combat vehicles to aid our troops, much less on horseback. Yet the Motor Transport Corps was formed during World War I to begin the transition of moving soldiers and supplies from Army horses to motorized vehicles.

Keep in mind that mass production of the motor car was a recent innovation by Henry Ford after the turn of the last century, and that Army horses outnumbered motorized vehicles by the thousands at that time. The teamwork involved to accomplish the eventual mechanization of the Army's transportation was a logistical marvel. By World War II the United States had the most mobile fighting machine in the world—organized planning at its finest. It's the kind of teamwork we all need to orchestrate to fulfill our definite chief aim or major purpose.

And what embodies enthusiasm better than "the kid" in this story, who drove the extra miles his job required every day through the life-threatening perils of the battlefield to support the troops? Then, caught up in the excitement of The National Pastime—baseball—he demanded the opposing pitcher in a pick-up game "stick it over," daring him to throw a strike. With shells exploding around him, his passion for baseball emboldened him to ignore mortal danger and crack a double—now THAT'S major league enthusiasm!

You see, during World War I, baseball was THE game in America. The NFL and NBA were not even formed yet. Babe Ruth was best known as a pitcher for the Boston Red Sox rather than a prolific Yankee home run hitter. There was no ESPN, no Sports Center, heck—no TV. There were no radio broadcasts of baseball games yet, and scant mention of them in newspapers. Yet baseball fever had been sweeping America since the mid-1800's in the sandlots, parks and playgrounds around the country. So "the kid" wasn't about to let a few enemy shells dampen his spirit for the game he loved—obviously he was made of "the right stuff." Imagine if you brought that same kind of enthusiasm to your world—what might you accomplish?

The Touchstone

George Harrison Phelps

The other day a salesman told me that all he needed was an opportunity. He made me think of Tagore's story of the wandering madman who searched for the magic stone, which would turn to gold all that it touched. Listen!

With matted locks, tawny and dust-laden, and body worn to a shadow, his lips tight pressed like the shut-up doors of his heart, his burning eyes like the lamp of a glow-worm seeking its mate—this was the wandering madman.

Before him the endless ocean roared.

The garrulous waves ceaselessly talked of hidden treasures, mocking the ignorance that knew not their meaning.

Maybe he now had no hope remaining, yet he would not rest, for search had become his life—

Just as the ocean forever lifts its arms to the sky for the unattainable—

Just as the stars go in circles, yet seeking a goal that can never be reached—

Even so on the lonely shore, the madman, with dusty, tawny locks, still roamed in search of the touchstone.

One day a village boy came up and asked, "Tell me, where did you come by this golden chain about your neck?"

The madman started—the chain that once was iron was verily gold; it was not a dream, but he did not know where it had changed. He struck his forehead wildly—where, oh, where, had he, without knowing it, achieved success?

It had grown into a habit to pick up pebbles and touch the chain, and to throw them away without looking to see if a change had come; thus the madman found and lost the touchstone.

The sun was sinking low in the west, the sky was of gold.

The madman returned on his footsteps to seek anew the lost treasure, with his strength gone, his body bent and his heart in the dust, like a tree uprooted.

Many a salesman has kicked the ladder of success from beneath his feet, just as the top rung was within his grasp. He was blinded to opportunity. He didn't recognize it when it came.

SEEING Opportunity—THAT'S THE SECRET.

Calumet Mine

Napoleon Hill

Thousands of people walked over the great Calumet Copper Mine without discovering it. Just one lone man used his "imagination," dug down into the earth a few feet, investigated, and discovered the richest copper deposit on earth.

You and every other person walk, at one time or another, over your "Calumet Mine." Discovery is a matter of investigation and use of "imagination." This course of the Fifteen Laws of Success may lead the way to your "Calumet," and you may be surprised when you discover that you were standing right over this rich mine, in the work in which you are now engaged. In his lecture on "Acres of Diamonds," Russell Conwell tells us that we need not seek opportunity in the distance; that we may find it right where we stand! THIS IS A TRUTH WELL WORTH REMEMBERING!

Source: *The Law of Success*. The Ralston University Press, 1928, Vol. I, Introduction: Personal Statement by the Author, last page.

The Wisdom of Knowing

Fr. Mike Morgera

Of all the Kings who ever lived and ruled; of all the leaders who ever led people into an unknown future; the quest for the touchstone goes on. The key to questions and answers is sought, found and lost in what seems a continuum of patterns in history. Environments and technologies change, but the patterns are endlessly repeated as leaders discover, learn and rule. Then other leaders forget, unlearn and rule.

A long time ago God said to a king, "Make a request of Me and I will grant it to you." The king said, "Give me wisdom and knowledge to lead this people, for otherwise who could rule this great people of Yours?" The king, whose name was Solomon, did not ask for rules, treasures, glory or revenge on his enemies. He asked for wisdom and knowledge. For a long time men have had the touchstone, but they forget. They find but lose the touchstone of wisdom and knowledge, only to seek it over and over.

Maybe someday they will find it and keep it and never throw it away and forget.

Grit

George Harrison Phelps

I sometimes wonder if we are not becoming bleached out in this sheltered life we lead. All the comforts and luxuries of a super-civilization and seldom the sharp sting of the elements against our white and tender skins.

I wonder sometimes if it wouldn't be good for us to turn loose in a blinding storm and let the rain and sleet wash off a bit of the perfume from the velvet of our hides. Let it make us smart and bleed and wince and grit our teeth—just to make men of us.

The other day I sat in the operating room of our hospital here at the works. A puny blister was interfering with my usual well-ordered and comfortable existence. As the interne was carefully binding up my wound the outer door opened and a workman entered, alone and unsupported. He was holding his right wrist in a grip of iron and I could see that his hand had been horribly crushed. Yet his face showed no emotion. It was stolid as a sphinx's face. He was laid on the operating table and left alone while the surgeon turned to get his instruments.

In a flash I saw that the man was fainting and I called to the doctor. After a few moments of heroic treatment the patient slowly opened his eyes and without a murmur submitted to the painful operation of dressing his wound.

When the work was completed he refused to remain and rest, but insisted on returning to his bench. He left the hospital unaided.

After he had gone, the surgeon turned to me and said, "That man will never have a closer call than he had a few moments ago. That wasn't a simple faint. He nearly died there on the table. His heart is bad and he has been out of the city hospital only a few days after a similar attack.

"And what's more, he knows what his trouble is. He's a 'He' MAN—that chap. God bless the breed. I wish we had more of them."

Those Who Can "Take It!"

Napoleon Hill

Those who can "take it" are bountifully rewarded for their PERSISTENCE. They receive, as their compensation, whatever goal they are pursuing. That is not all! They receive something infinitely more important than material compensation—the knowledge that "EVERY FAILURE BRINGS WITH IT THE SEED OF AN EQUIVALENT ADVANTAGE."

There are no exceptions to this rule; a few people know from experience the soundness of persistence. They are the ones who have not accepted defeat as being anything more than temporary. They are the ones whose DESIRES are so PERSISTENTLY APPLIED that defeat is finally changed into victory. We who stand on the side-lines of Life see the overwhelmingly large number who go down in defeat, never to rise again. We see the few who take the punishment of defeat *as an urge to greater effort*. These, fortunately, never learn to accept Life's reverse gear. But what we DO NOT SEE, what most of us never suspect of existing, is the silent but irresistible POWER which comes to the rescue of those who fight on in the face of discouragement. If we speak of this power at all we call it PERSISTENCE, and let it go at that. One thing we all know, if one does not possess PERSISTENCE, one does not achieve noteworthy success in any calling.

Source: *Think and Grow Rich*. The Ralston Society, 1937, p. 230.

Service

George Harrison Phelps

From Egypt and the Sacred White Bull of Apis to Boston and Christian Science we have had religions and rituals without number. During the last fifty years we have evolved in the business world a real religion without form, or code, or dogma; a religion of the head as well as of the heart—the Religion of Service.

In olden days the leaders in the religion of service were the high priests, the philosophers, the monks and the knights-at-arms. They moulded the best thought of the time; they saved art and learning from the night of the Middle Ages; they gave the world ideals; they fought for justice and honneur and courtesie.

The modern business man has the power of the high priest, the foresight of the philosopher, the skill of the monk and the spirit of the knight-at-arms. He produces the best possible goods at the lowest possible prices. Thru the inevitable laws of right he is bringing justice to a people that had forgotten justice. Thru the medium of publicity he is bringing honor and the courtesy that compels attention and respect to a world whose motto for a thousand years had been *"Caveat Emptor!"*—"Let the Buyer Beware!"

Our great business man of today started with but a shrewd head, a heart of invincible courage, a soul of mighty vision. Thru long years of self-denial and patient toil, giving over his youth and all fair beckoning shapes of Folly, he has at last come—his hair silvered by Time—to the realization of his vision, splendid beyond wildest imagining. He has come to that peace which is born of perfect giving, joyously and with power fulfilling a world's desire. The day of hell-fire and eternal damnation, the day of the "leather chair" philosopher is done. This is the age of the man who acts. The doers of the world are crowned. He has the greatest power who most effectively serves his fellowmen.

Strange, is it not, that the greatest figure in the world's greatest religion should say, "Greater love hath no man that this, that he lay down his life for his friends." The religion he foresaw was a religion of the here and now, a religion not of services, but of service.

The businessmen of America have above all others contributed to the comfort, safety and conveniences of the people. They have been the servants of humanity, the prophets, the builders of the better day. They have made a science of salesmanship. They have raised advertising to the dignity of literature and art. They have made a living religion of that sublime command, "The greatest among you shall be your servant."

They have come to understand that life is not the mere conquest of material things—the scramble, the clutching, the toiling for money and power—but that real happiness can be attained only thru efficient service; service to each other in their daily problems and perplexities; service as an organization to those with whom they deal.

All happy, hard-working, efficient manufacturers, distributors, salesmen and advertisers are members of this mighty church, the Men who serve their World.

This is their single purpose. "Every customer must make a profit when he buys, and that profit must be absolute satisfaction."

The Experiment

Napoleon Hill

During the next six months make it your business to render useful service to at least one person every day, for which you neither expect nor accept monetary pay.

Go at this experiment with faith that it will uncover for your use one of the most powerful laws that enter into the achievement of enduring success, and you will not be disappointed.

The rendering of this service may take on any one of more than a score of forms. For example, it may be rendered personally to one or more specific persons; or it may be rendered to your employer, in the nature of work that you perform after hours.

Again, it may be rendered to entire strangers whom you never expect to see again. It matters not to whom you render this service so long as you render it with willingness, and solely for the purpose of benefiting others.

If you carry out this experiment in the proper attitude of mind, you will discover that which all others who have become familiar with the law upon which it is based have discovered; namely, that—

> *You can no more render service without receiving compensation than you can withhold the rendering of it without suffering the loss of reward.*

"Cause and effect, means and ends, seed and fruit, cannot be severed," says Emerson; "for the effect already blooms in the cause, the end pre-exists in the means, the fruit in the seed."

Source: *The Law of Success.* The Ralston University Press, 1928, Vol. V, p. 113.

Service — The Golden Rule in Action

Raymond Campbell

Implicit in the concept of service is action. You cannot perform or provide a service without taking action. And it's as true today as it was one hundred years ago that your actions will speak volumes about you. Action is also at the heart of the Golden Rule: Do unto others as you would have others do unto to you. As a kind of mantra, the Golden Rule should guide your decision-making. It will also repay your choices with consequences that are perfectly in line with the nature of the decisions you make.

The Golden Rule is closely related to Personal Initiative and its twin brother the Law of Going the Extra Mile — two of the seventeen principles of success taught by Napoleon Hill in the Science of Personal Achievement. The very act of rendering more service than you are paid to render puts into operation the Law of Attraction which is the same law that forms the basis of the Golden Rule.

The foresight of the philosopher ... the very word *philosopher* is derived from two Greek words *philo* and *sophia* meaning love and truth. A philosopher is the lover of truth. The business person of the 21st century is a modern day philosopher, one who understands the Golden Rule, does not confuse today's profit with a lifetime of success and peace of mind. One who knows that success is measured by the sum total of all actions, not by a series of separate actions.

Dr. Hill believed that the truly educated person (not someone with a higher education) knew how to get whatever he wanted in life "without violating the Laws of God, the Laws of Man, or the Rights of Others." He will not, therefore, take unfair advantage of anyone, for he knows that every act will reward itself either positively or negatively. He understands that the single purpose of business is that—"Every customer must make a profit when he buys, and that profit must be absolute satisfaction."

In all your dealings, have the foresight of a philosopher, recognize the rights of others, and daily apply the Golden Rule; let your actions speak louder than words, and you shall be rewarded with prosperity and peace of mind.

Joe Hawk

George Harrison Phelps

Courtesy and kindliness are as essential to the business of selling as faith in God is to the business of preaching the gospel.

Be courteous always. It opens the heart and mind of the man with whom you deal. It predisposes him in your favor. It is the open sesame of salesmanship.

Every time I see a fresh young salesman bluster about and blurt along without stopping to think who comes within range of his words, I think of the wise young soul who knew everything about anything that ever was or would be, who sank his frame neck deep in the mire of embarrassment by a few things of derision which he regarded as funny.

It happened that this young man found a wire when he arrived at his hotel in a western town one evening, ordering him to an Arizona station several hundred miles farther south. Joe Hawk, a wealthy and influential citizen, said the message, was waiting to discuss an order for several thousand dollars worth of goods. It was a big chance for a big deal. The salesman started on the journey at once. On the train he made the acquaintance of another young man who chanced to be bound for the same town. The two got off the train together.

But for the silent figure of a stalwart Indian, sitting on a truck at the end of the platform, the station seemed deserted. Anticipation of a fat order with little effort put the salesman in an effervescent mood. "Ugh, heap big chief, bow-wow!" he remarked as he and his companion passed the Indian. The red-skin never moved a muscle. Even the faint expression of contempt that stole over his swarthy visage was not perceptible to the salesmen. They laughed at his silence and the man who sought the order turned again to repeat his derisive greeting. It was then the station master, overhearing the jibes, approached and laid his hand gently on the salesman's shoulder. "Young man," he said, "it might interest you to know that this Indian is a scholar and a gentleman. He is a graduate of Carlisle University, with several degrees, and is one of the wealthiest landowners in this section of the west."

The salesman turned meekly on his informant. The flush of shame on his face gave way to a sudden pallor. He almost gasped—"Who is he—this man? His name?"

"Hawk," said the station master. "That's Joe Hawk."

The best thing the years bring is the knowledge that courtesy and kindliness, plus direct and dynamic selling power, is the formula that wins.

The King of Kings came among men as an humble carpenter of Nazareth.

The gods oft appear in disguise to try men's souls. Farmers in overalls are the best prospects in the world.

Essential courtesy and kindliness are predominating characteristics of all successful salesmen.

Be courteous. Be kind.

Blinded by Prejudice

Napoleon Hill

Do not judge a man by what his enemies say about him, because they are apt to be blinded by prejudice. If you want the true measure of a man find out if he loves flowers and music and little children. Find out if he is interested in nature's handiwork as it is interpreted in the green grass and the flowing brooks and singing birds, for there can be NO GREAT WRONG with a man who love these.

As a final test, find out if he has evolved to where he forgives those who wrong him and does not slander those whom he does not like. And, if he is married and has children, find out if he is a hero in their estimation, or, whether his homecoming is marked by fear and trembling. There is something radically wrong about a man whose wife and children do not greet him with a hearty welcome.

Source: *Napoleon Hill's Magazine*, July, 1921, back cover.

Let Us Give Thanks

George Harrison Phelps

It is a law of nature that nothing is at a stand-still. We are better men today than we were yesterday—or we are worse. We either advance or we decline. Power comes from looking forward with faith and courage—of expecting and demanding better things. We can't go forward by looking backward.

In the world's business of today our successful merchants, our enterprising, pushing men of affairs spend little time with the memories of their bygone struggles. They live ahead of their business. Nature buries its dead with little delay. The tree produces new foliage with each new season and treasures up no withered leaves to bring back memories of other days. Success and happiness is never gained by looking backward.

Nearly three hundred years ago a little band of fifty-five stern men, surrounded by savages, faced a winter of sickness and starvation—and looked back upon a year of hardship and death. This land of ours had given a shabby welcome to these Pilgrim Fathers and they had little to look forward to as the second winter came upon them with half their intrepid company already buried underneath the snows. Their harvests had failed them and the game had left their forests. Yet they sat down to that first Thanksgiving with faith and hope and enthusiasm in their breasts. They looked ahead for better things to come, determined to forget those dreary months of toil and disappointment. Little they realized what those prayers would bring.

Many Thanksgivings have come and gone since those pioneers of progress tramped the unmarked trails of tangled wilderness. These hand-hewn paths have now widened into broad highways. The spires of a nation have reared themselves from out the silence of that autumn long ago. And yet again today emerging from the world's most terrible conflict a hundred million people are marching on in uncounted wealth to greater prosperity, greater civilization, greater happiness.

Truly, all this is a fitting monument to the simple faith and courage of those rugged men who turned their backs upon their sorrows and built anew—the foundations of a New World.

YOUR opportunity is here—right now—

What are YOU going to do with it?

Nature's Plan

Napoleon Hill

I am convinced that failure is Nature's plan through which she hurdle-jumps men of destiny and prepares them to do their work. Failure is Nature's great crucible in which she burns the dross from the human heart and so purifies the metal of the man that it can stand the test of hard usage.

I have found evidence to support this theory in the study of the records of scores of great men, from Socrates and Christ on down the centuries to the well-known men of achievement of our modern times. The success of each man seemed to be in almost exact ratio to the extent of the obstacles and difficulties he had to surmount.

No man ever arose from the knock-out blow of defeat without being stronger and wiser for the experience. Defeat talks to us in a language all its own; a language to which we must listen whether we like it or not.

Source: *The Law of Success.* The Ralston University Press, 1928, Vol. VIII, pp. 43–44.

Color

George Harrison Phelps

Your business takes its color from your soul. Merchant, salesman, mechanic—it makes no difference who you are or what you do. The character of your work is measured by the materials of your body and your brain that go to make it live. Until you make yourself a part of the thing you do—just so long you will do but little.

The world is never fooled. It recognizes sincerity and knows what manner of men we are.

"How can you expect me to hear what you say," asks Emerson, "when what you ARE keeps thundering in my ears?"

"A man's work is but an expression of the character of the man; so is a man made in the image of the work he does."

Olive Schreiner tells the story of an artist whose life was painted into his picture:

"Other artists had colors richer and rarer, and painted more notable pictures. He painted his with one color; there was a wonderful red glow in it; and the people went up and down saying, 'We like the picture; we like the glow.'

"The other artists came and said, 'Where does he get his color from?' They asked him, and he smiled and said, 'I cannot tell you,' and worked on with his head bent low.

"And one went to the Far East and brought costly pigments and made a rare color and painted, but after a time the picture faded. Another read in the old books, and made a color rich and rare, but when he put it on the picture, it was dead.

"But the artist painted on. Always the work grew redder and redder and the artist grew whiter and whiter. At last one day they found him dead before his picture, and they took him up to bury him. The other men looked about in all the pots and crucibles, but they found nothing they had not.

"And when they undressed him and put his grave-clothes on him, they found above his left breast a mark of a wound—it was an old, old wound, that must have been there all his life, for the edges were old and hardened; but Death, who seals all things, had drawn the edges together and closed it up.

"And they buried him. And still the people went about saying, 'Where did he get his color from?'"

And it came to pass that after a while the artist was forgotten—BUT THE WORK LIVED.

Desire

Napoleon Hill

It is believed by men who have devoted years of research to the subject, that all energy and matter throughout the universe respond to and are controlled by the Law of Attraction which causes elements and forces of a similar nature to gather around certain centers of attraction. It is through the operation of this same universal Law of Attraction that constant, deeply seated, strong DESIRE attracts the physical equivalent or counterpart of the thing desired, or the means of securing it.

We have learned, then, if this hypothesis is correct, that all cycles of human achievement work somewhat after this fashion: First, we picture in our conscious minds, through a definite chief aim (based upon a strong desire), some objective;

we then focus our conscious mind upon this objective, by constant thought of it and belief in its attainment, until the subconscious section of the mind takes up the picture or outline of this objective and impels us to take the necessary physical action to transform that picture into reality.

Source: *The Law of Success*. The Ralston University Press, 1928, Vol. VI, pp. 109, 111.

The Color Red

Michael Telapary

Color is one of the greatest gifts of nature to humankind. Color awakens in us the mysterious energies that we call emotions. Nature is filled with color, so are the pictures of all our experiences and visualizations we carry in our subconscious minds. It is a little known fact that our brains have a tendency to bring colors into a harmonious neutral gray. In order to achieve this, our brain uses a complementary color. For example, if we look at the color red, our brain mixes it with its complementary color green which will turn the mixture to a neutral gray. This then gives us the feeling of harmony, balance, happiness and satisfaction, feelings we all strive for in our lives. All we think and do in our life has no value or meaning if it can't be perceived by other human beings.

Napoleon Hill's first principle, Definiteness of Purpose, is one of the most important principles to master if you are intending to get the success you want in your life. By putting a definite aim into your mind, mixed with a definite plan that you are going to give in return to achieve it, is giving your mind the task of bringing everything into harmony along your path towards that definite purpose. Dr. Hill says you have to make it a burning desire until it becomes an obsession. In this way the visualization of your definite purpose will be imprinted on your subconscious mind. In turn your subconscious mind will hand over new plans and ideas to you in the form of sudden opportunities and hunches, for you to grab and work with, in order to get you closer to your definite purpose.

The artist in Olive Schreiner's story used several of Dr. Hill's principles of success. To try to understand the reasons why this man could make those wonderful paintings, that triggered the emotions of the observers, we have to go back in his past and imagine the experience he had that left the scar on his breast. During his early life he lost his beloved wife in a battle, which almost took his own life as well. His mind was filled with this happening and for years and years he could only experience grief. Life held no meaning for him anymore. Then he finally realized that he should be grateful because he was still alive for a purpose. He decided to transform his former negative feeling into a positive one. From then on he had but only one major definite purpose in life and that was to serve as many people as possible in the world by giving them a feeling of love and happiness. He choose to make that happen through his paintings. Thus by making use of the first principle, Definiteness of Purpose, he had made his first step towards the realization of his dream.

His burning desire to succeed was there from the start. When he used the principle of Applied Faith together with the eternal love for his lost loved one, this mixture of high energy gave his power of thought a much higher rate of vibration than normal. Dr. Hill says that this higher vibration of thought energy enables the subconscious mind to connect to a universal intelligence which he calls "Infinite Intelligence."

This external source of knowledge gave the artist's subconscious mind the ability to create the right ideas to let the man create his mysterious paintings that radiated all those wonderful emotions to the spectators. He could only think in the color red, which is the color of blood but also the color of love. The genius inside helped him to create the right atmosphere in his paintings. This man made use of several other principles. He had built a "positive mental attitude" which helped him to transform his negative thinking from the past into a positive one. He was willing to "go the extra mile" by going beyond where other artists would stop. Finally he used "self-discipline" to paint until he reached his definite purpose. When he died he became one with his art. No wonder his fellow artists never found his secret: it was hidden in his mind and vanished when he died.

The Lavender Merchant

George Harrison Phelps

How often we have heard the old, old law that men of success gravitate naturally toward each other! And yet how seldom we give it consideration. It is not mere superstition that makes one avoid a failure. Like a magnet, a successful man or a successful institution throws out an unseen force for greater power.

Look successful; don't be satisfied with the commonplace. The world has catalogued you at the price you mark on your own tag. The personal appearance of a salesman is a dominant factor in any sale. So merchandise is judged largely by the appearance of the place in which it is bought.

The more money one spends wisely in making a place of business attractive, the more and better class of customers it will attract.

The fashionable haberdasher locates his shop on the best business thorofare, pays a high rent, decorates his window attractively and employs only the best and most courteous salesmen. By this method he attracts the best trade. This is a law of success that is followed in all parts of the world. In village or city, it still holds good. It is as important to the country merchant as to the capitalist. Human nature is no different in Boston than it is in Brighton, Mich.

Before the earthquake the Blind Lavender Merchant of San Francisco was almost as well known locally as the Golden

Gate. "He could have sold shoestrings or lead pencils," said the San Francisco Bulletin, "but he did not. He could have bid for sympathy and nickels by making the air strident with song or hand-organ. Instead he made himself a picturesque institution. The Lavender Merchant was as historical of old San Francisco as the flower market, the old Palace Court and former Chinatown. He always constituted a distinctive bit of color at the edge of the most exclusive shopping district."

Faithful and patient as the statue in the park, he stood from dawn till dusk in the midst of costly laces and satins and silks. Luxuries his sightless and disfigured eyes could never see. His little shop was only a dark mahogany stained box strung by a leathern strap about his neck, its lid thrown wide. On a violet background in white scroll letters, "Genuine English Lavender, 10 cents a package," was announced for sale. In the bottom of the tray prepared packages in neat little manila envelopes reposed in a bed of dried pale lilac blossoms, making the air aromatic for blocks, and conjuring visions of old-fashioned closets piled high with snowy linen and old chests filled with worn laces and wedding gowns treasured in lavender against moths and destruction, because of some delicate sentiment or romance.

It seemed that San Francisco never was and never could be, when the blind lavender merchant was not.

Yes—he could have sold shoestrings—or pencils—or chewing gum—or a dozen other gee-gaws, but he did not. Instead he used his imagination and decorated his business to appeal to those with whom he had to deal. He applied one of the basic laws of salesmanship—the law of attractiveness.

Take a moment right now for critical inspection of YOURSELF and YOUR place of business. THEN WADE IN AND RENOVATE.

An Attractive Personality

Napoleon Hill

An attractive personality usually may be found in the person who speaks gently and kindly, selecting words which do not offend; who selects clothing of appropriate style and colors which harmonize; who is unselfish and willing to serve others; who is a friend of all humanity, regardless of politics, religion, creed or economic viewpoints; who refrains from speaking unkindly of others, either with or without cause; who manages to converse without being drawn into an argument or trying to draw others into argument on such debatable subjects as religion and politics; who sees the good there is in people and overlooks the bad; who seeks neither to reform nor reprimand others; who smiles frequently and deeply; who loves little children, flowers, birds, the growing grass, the trees and the running brooks; who sympathizes with all who are in trouble; who forgives acts of unkindness; who willingly grants to others the rights to do as they please as long as no one else's rights are interfered with; who earnestly strives to be constructive in every thought and act; who encourages others and spurs them on to greater undertakings in some useful work for the good of humanity, by interesting them in themselves and inspiring them with self-confidence; who is a patient and interested listener and makes a habit of giving the other person a part of the conversation without breaking in and doing all the talking.

Source: *Napoleon Hill's Magazine*, April, 1921, p. 35.

The Lavender Merchant: Choice and Definite Chief Aim

Christina Chia

"As we thinketh in our heart so are we." This famous quote which can be found in the Bible and in many books reminds us that we are what we think all day long. The first chapter of Dr. Napoleon Hill's classic book *Think and Grow Rich* is entitled "Thoughts are things." Indeed everything begins with a seed of thought. We all have the power to choose our thoughts. According to Dr. Hill in *Law of Success* having a definite chief aim is the starting point of all achievement.

The blind Lavender Merchant understood that success breeds success and success attracts more success. Instead of yielding to the circumstances of life, he did not resign to accept his fate and do what people in his shoes would have done and that is selling shoestrings or lead pencils. He had a definite chief aim to build a business selling Lavender in an up market place. He uses his imagination to package his product and decorate his place of business. Albert Einstein said "Imagination is more powerful than knowledge." Dr. Napoleon Hill had constantly reminded us in his teachings that thought is the only thing which we have absolute control and imagination is for our free use. We either used it or lose it.

I have learned from my snorkeling experience in the marine park in Tioman Island in Malaysia that we have to go to where the fishes are. I bought a bag of breads to feed the fishes. I saw the area near the jetty was crowded with people and I decided to move to a place where there are fewer people. I thought I would have all the fishes to myself. Little did I know that there were not many fishes in the areas that were not so crowded. I did not have takers for my bread. When I decided to go back to the jetty area, I saw scores of fishes all around me and within seconds my bag of breads were gone. Looks like the Lavender man did the right thing by using his personal initiative to set up business in the area where the more affluence people are.

The Lavender Merchant is also saturating his mind with success consciousness by dressing his business like a success and be among laces and satins. Our subconscious mind is like a garden. It will accept what we put in and give to us exactly what we sow. By being in the right place, the Lavender man is attracting the right people who will appreciate his products.

The Lavender Merchant also exhibits self confidence, persistence and positive mental attitude. I recalled Dr. Hill makes a comparison between a man on a wheel chair whom he frequently saw in New York city begging for a living, while at the same time there is another man who is also in a wheel chair and in the same condition as this man who is the President of America. Life is about choices. The choices we make will create the outcome of our life. We are all creatures of habit. We can choose to have success habits or failure habits. What will you choose?

Andrew Jackson

George Harrison Phelps

Have you ever watched a Marathon and seen a little, unknown athlete throw back his head, pull in his elbows and spurt for a winning finish, beating the champion runner to the tape? Have you ever stood up in the grandstand and cheered until your throat was parched, as the losing team, answering the call of its captain, braced up in the last two minutes of play and made plunge after plunge toward the goal?

You know the thrill that comes as you see a horse that takes the whip and stands a drive at the finish. It is courage that you cheer for—courage and pluck and nerve. The world's prizes go to those who have the courage.

There are no blue ribbons for the cowards.

One morning, a long time ago, when Andrew Jackson was a young judge in Tennessee, a notorious bully started a disturbance in the court room. Jackson ordered the marshal to arrest him and place him in confinement. The task, however, proved to be a difficult one, as the bully backed into a corner and threatened to shoot the first man that moved.

The marshal hesitated and lost his nerve. The bully was master of the scene. "Call a posse," said the judge, "and rush him; he's afraid to shoot." Again the bully raised his gun and every man stood still. A smile of derision spread over Jackson's face. "Court is adjourned for three minutes," he thundered. "Marshal, call on me."

Without a weapon Jackson left the bench and marched straight toward the barrel of the gun. The court room held its breath as the bully crouched a little and raised the hammer of his pistol—but Jackson never faltered. The bully saw only courage and determination in the judge's face. He knew he had met his master.

He dropped his gun and wilted.

Courage commands respect. It won for us in our schoolboy games and it wins in the game of life. When business comes the hardest and the prospect list gets low—put on your boots and wade out through the drifts. You'll be surprised at what grows underneath the snow.

Right now make up your mind.

Courage will win.

This Demon Called Fear

Napoleon Hill

The development of self-confidence starts with the elimination of this demon called fear, which sits upon a man's shoulder and whispers into his ear, "You can't do it—you are afraid to try—you are afraid of public opinion—you are afraid that you will fail—you are afraid you have not the ability."

This fear demon is getting into close quarters. Science has found a deadly weapon with which to put it to flight, and this lesson on self-confidence has brought you this weapon for use in your battle with the world-old enemy of progress, fear.

Source: *The Law of Success*. The Ralston University Press, 1928, Vol. II, pp. 72–73.

Courage in Adversity

John Garcia

The history of mankind is full of examples of individuals who have made the world a better place through acts of courage and bravery. Some of them, such as the soldier who casts himself onto an exploding grenade to save the lives of his fellow squad members, are big and noteworthy. Some others, such as the child who walks into the darkness to turn the light on to see by herself there is no monster under her bed, may seem small and go almost unnoticed. However, in each case, fear was conquered and a victorious soul emerged from the realms of mediocrity and weakness.

Every one of us has been or surely will be in front of a seemingly insurmountable situation: the death of a loved one, an oral presentation in front of a very important client, a poor business decision that eventually led to bankruptcy, the cruel actions of a bully that is picking on us, a very difficult academic test, etc. When confronted by any of these difficult issues, Dr. Napoleon Hill's 17 Principles of Personal Achievement may provide you with beautiful and powerful insight into the type of actions and mindset that will help you cope with your difficulties successfully and conquer your fears and anxieties. Enthusiasm, Positive Mental Attitude, Self-Discipline and Learning from Adversity and Defeat are potent concepts that when applied can change your life because of their effect over your perception, and perception is reality.

In the face of a very frightful, unintended situation, Pres. Jackson was able to stay calm and find a solution to the situation he faced. I'm convinced he developed that ability over the course of time by making a conscious effort to stay in control of his fate, not the other way around. You can learn and apply the same principles in your own life. I am sure you can, because you have.

Stop for a moment and think back to a situation in which you experienced fear, but a higher motivation or desire helped you come back to your senses and look up to Heaven imploring for help; then you were able to face the problem with a combination of your own ability and the Divine strength. Developing this attitude when confronted with adversity might be far from easy, and acquiring it may require both time and effort from you. From my own experience, I have learned that personal growth is often excruciating, but the transformation and improvement you will experience by going through this process are worth the pain.

And just as others have been a source of inspiration to you because of their courage and self-control, you can also inspire others by moving forward with optimism, enthused by a higher objective, even in the midst of pain, danger, fear, stress, affliction and desperation to conquer your own Goliaths, like David of old.

Kitchener

George Harrison Phelps

Not many weeks ago he was in exultant spirits. There was a big demand and money was coming easily. His only trouble was the fact that he was selling more merchandise than he could get. Then, one day as the Autumn mornings again turned from crisp to cold and everyone seemed full of energy and determination, I got a letter from him—an apologetic kind of a letter—full of excuses. He'd quit—thrown up his hands right in the middle of the Fall selling season, and quit. "Crops were a failure," he said, and anyway there was no use trying to push business again until Spring—the selling season was over.

We had always thought of him as a real merchandiser, but now we knew that he had lost his nerve. His backbone was gone.

He was a poor fighter.

There is a great lesson for this merchant in the inspiring accounts of the life, the work, and the fighting spirit of one of the most prominent figures in the war. Lord Kitchener was one of the greatest fighters that our time has known.

Since that tragic day when the cruiser Hampshire went down, and a raft was flung ashore with only twelve men clinging to it—and Kitchener not among them—the words of his life creed have reverberated to the far corners of the civilized world.

"We will always need and will always have soldiers," he said. "They are absolutely essential in the highest civilization.

Without the military spirit, nations decay. WITHOUT THE FIGHTING SPIRIT, A NATION—OR A MAN—WILL ROT."

In all his work, whether as warrior or as pioneer, Kitchener's persistence and fighting spirit put him in the class of superman. At the time he started out to avenge Gordon's death, some twenty years ago, he began the construction of a railroad from Cairo to Khartoum. The roadbed was surveyed through a desert from Halfa to Abu Hamed, 230 miles without an oasis. He was ridiculed all over the British Empire. The entire carrying capacity of the train would be taken up by the water supply necessary for the locomotive. But they reckoned without the fighting spirit stowed away inside this man of iron will. Kitchener pushed on and one day alone saw 5,300 yards of iron ribbons strung across the burning sands. The work was finished.

To Kitchener, fighting meant only training men and equipping them with ammunition for every emergency, placing them in position where they could not lose, and placing the enemy in position where he could not win.

So, when business looks bad and crops fail and the frosts come—remember Kitchener.

Fight—don't lose your nerve!

Self-Confidence Formula

Napoleon Hill

1. I know that I have the ability to achieve the object of my definite purpose in life; therefore, I demand of myself persistent, continuous action toward its attainment, and I here and now promise to render such action.
2. I realize the dominating thoughts of my mind will eventually reproduce themselves in outward, physical action, and gradually transform themselves into physical reality; therefore, I will concentrate my thought, for thirty minutes daily, upon the task of thinking of the person I intend to become, thereby creating in my mind a clear mental picture.
3. I know through the principle of autosuggestion, any desire that I persistently hold in my mind will eventually seek expression through some practical means of attaining the object back of it; therefore, I will devote ten minutes daily to demanding of myself the development of self-confidence.
4. I have clearly written down a description of my definite chief aim in life, and I will never stop trying, until I shall have developed sufficient self-confidence for its attainment.
5. I fully realize that no wealth or position can long endure, unless built upon truth and justice; therefore, I will engage in no transaction that does not benefit all whom it affects. I will succeed by attracting to myself the forces I wish to use, and the cooperation of other people. I will induce others to serve me, because of my willingness to serve others. I will eliminate hatred,

> envy, jealousy, selfishness, and cynicism, by developing love for all humanity, because I know that a negative attitude toward others can never bring me success. I will cause others to believe in me, because I will believe in them, and in myself. I will sign my name to this formula, commit it to memory, and repeat it aloud once a day, with full faith that it will gradually influence my thoughts and actions so that I will become a self-reliant, and successful, person.

Back of this formula is a law of nature that no man has yet been able to explain. The name by which one calls this law is of little importance. The important fact about it is—it works for the glory and success of mankind, if it is used constructively. On the other hand, if used destructively, it will destroy just as readily. In this statement may be found a very significant truth, namely, that those who go down in defeat, and end their lives in poverty, misery, and distress, do so because of negative application of the principle of autosuggestion. The cause may be found in the fact that all impulses of thought have a tendency to clothe themselves in their physical equivalent.

Source: *Think and Grow Rich*. The Ralston Society, 1937, pp. 74–76.

Burbank

George Harrison Phelps

The instinctive judgment of the public seldom errs. It will sense the little insincerities, the little discourtesies, the little exaggerations as quickly as the mother feels the approaching danger to her child.

"If you would pass down the western slope of life unlonely, with friends to make your last days round and full, guard well the subtle influence of your personality on those you meet today," says Thoreau.

As it is with life, so it is with business. The seemingly insignificant things are often the most important. Sometimes we may feel that a little white lie, a bit of idle gossip, a broken promise really does no lasting harm. But every thought we think, every deed we do, every promise we make, either strengthens or weakens the fabric of our business. Just as a tiny drop of aniline dye will color a whole hogshead of water, so will the carelessness of these little things color the opinion in which we are held by those with whom we deal.

Out in Santa Rosa, the wonderful botanical gardens of Luther Burbank are carefully guarded, but one day the gate was left open and a little girl peering through, could not resist the temptation to take a lily growing near the wall. There was only one blossom on the stalk—all the others had gone to seed. In her haste to pluck the flower she stripped the stalk of the ripened pods and the seeds were scattered in the sand and gravel.

A short time afterwards, as Mr. Burbank was walking through the garden, he missed the lily. In dismay he realized that the work of years was wasted. With tears streaming down his cheeks he called to his sister and the two went back to hunt for the seeds in the trodden sand. There, on his hands and knees, the famous Burbank searched patiently, hour after hour, until the tiny seeds—the almost invisible objects of his painful effort—had been recovered.

To the little girl the flower as a minor thing—pretty, fit to be plucked. To Burbank it was a wonderful achievement, based on endless hours of toil and experimentation. Her thoughtless delight at thus finding a lily to wear was to him a grave misfortune. Little wonder he wept.

As easily as the child wrecked the creation to which Burbank had given years, so may a man wreck and despoil the principle of his business. A careless word, a little "knock," a bit of subterfuge, and dry rot has started on its way.

It's these little things under which foundations crumble. Watch them!

Golden Rule Thoughts!

Napoleon Hill

> *"There is something as rotten as hell about the man who is always trying to show the other fellow up."–Billy Sunday*

One of the most destructive evils in this world is slanderous talk. It breaks human hearts and ruins reputations with a ruthlessness unknown of all other evils.

Slander resembles a double-edged sword—it cuts going and coming. It not only undermines the one slandered, but, it comes back like a boomerang and gnaws at the reputation of the slanderer as well. The slanderer soon becomes accustomed to seeing only the petty sides of others. Little by little he bathes his own soul in the foulness of his own thoughts and words until he cannot see the beauty in anything or anyone.

He measures everything by his own perverted standard. Take notice of those who slander or engage in any sort of suggestive evil speaking about others and you will see, as clearly as you can see the sun on a bright day, that their words are but a confession of their own heart secrets. The faults which we find in our neighbors most readily are usually but a reflection of our own weaknesses.

A man only begins to be a man when he ceases to whine and revile, and commences to search for the hidden justice which regulates his life. And as he adapts his mind to that regulating factor, he ceases to accuse others as the cause of his unhappy condition, and builds himself up in strong and noble thoughts. He ceases to kick against circumstances, stops finding fault with his neighbors, and begins to discover the hidden powers and possibilities within himself.

Here is a test that you can apply to yourself with profit: The next time the name of someone whom you dislike is mentioned in your presence see if you can either hold your tongue or speak no evil of that person. If you meet the test you have reason to be proud of yourself because you are vitalizing your personality with that peculiar brand of magnetism which will attract the best people of your neighborhood to you.

You do not attract that which you want, but that which you harbor in your own heart; in fact that which you are! This is in accordance with a well-established principle which never varies. Through the operation of this principle, which is nothing more or less than the Golden Rule, you can rise to the heights in any position; you can attract customers or clients in any business or profession; you can make permanent friends of all whom you know, and, best of all, you can fill your own heart with self-respect and happiness which none who look for the meanness in other people ever experience. You can get any person to act toward you as you wish him to act by first acting that same way toward him, and then keeping at it until he responds in kind, which will be sooner than you might imagine. Try it.

Source: *Napoleon Hill's Magazine*. September, 1921, p. 37.

Learn From Adversity and Defeat

Sr. Deborah Davis, PHJC

While little things can undermine one's business or one's personal life, it's also the little things, if seen in the right perspective, which can strengthen beliefs, animate one for challenges ahead or reaffirm convictions. The seemingly insignificant can take on importance if we but pay attention to them. Even our small set-backs or defeats can serve us well; can provide "teachable moments" for us. For Luther Burbank, getting down on his hands and knees to retrieve his dream gives form to one of the 17 Principles of Success, "Learn From Adversity and Defeat." Though devastated by the insensitive action of the child, the world famous botanist moved forward, repossessing his vision and developing more than 800 varieties of hybridized plants. This lily-plucking girl created a problem, and he found the solution.

In another century and in another country, the story of learning from defeat continues. Maria Elena, an indigenous woman from central Mexico, could have faced her childhood of neglect and abuse by giving up on herself and on life. Raised in a one room house made of large stones stacked one on top of the other, she and her four sisters were denied formal education. The five brothers were all allowed to go the school. Her father's belief was that girls only needed to learn how to grind the corn and how to make their tortillas. Sending girls to school was a waste of time and precious money. Typical of her indigenous group and that period of time, she began having her own children at the age of 15. After the birth of her fourth child, all girls, her husband first brutally beat her, causing the loss of her right eye. He then left her to look for a woman who could give him sons. Maria Elena chose not to view this as a stumbling block but rather as a stepping stone, for her own liberation and that of her daughters. Through her many years of forfeiting luxuries, and never giving up, she refused to accept defeat as permanent. She declined to recognize the harsh conditions of her poverty as failure. Though she would not have used the phrase, her "positive mental attitude" brought her through. With the necessary sacrifices that a mother makes, Maria Elena insisted that all four girls attend first elementary school, then high school. At this writing, two of the four have completed university, and are professional women while the other two are finishing their formal education. And, in not accepting limitations and defeat in her own life, Maria Elena herself has begun literacy classes. She takes delight in proving her father wrong, that she can do far more than grind corn and make tortillas. She has in fact, like the 19th century botanist, learned from adversity and defeat.

It's Up to You

George Harrison Phelps

The product of an institution is never superior to its dominating personality. Your business is the reflection of your temperament. As YOU think, so will your employees think. YOU are the thermostat of your organization.

You are a fountain of inspiration or you are a drag on initiative. You impel your men by your strength of purpose or you retard them by your physical and mental sluggishness. They breathe your atmosphere. They get your viewpoint. They thrive—or they rot.

Washington had only to appear before his troops and instantly despair was changed to wild enthusiasm. It has been said that men are always greedy for emotion. Enthusiasm is largely a matter of appealing to that "greed." A resourceful dealer never lets enthusiasm lag.

It was not the Roman army that conquered Gaul—it was Caesar. It was not the soldiers of Carthage that held the Republican army trembling at the gates of Rome—it was Hannibal. It is not your sales department that breaks a record or strikes a rut—it's YOU!

Several years ago the *London Times* told the following story of a stampede of Russian cavalry:

"On the second night of the campaign an unlucky accident occurred. A regiment of the Empress' Cuirassiers of the Guard, 900 strong, had arrived at their cantonments. One of the squadrons of horses became alarmed, broke away, was followed by the next squadron and, a panic seizing them all, in one instant the whole 900 fled in wild disorder. When I tell you that some of the horses were not recovered until they had gone into Finland you may imagine what the panic was. In one solid mass they dashed on for miles and then came directly at right angles to a river. In front of them was a bridge, but on the other side of the bridge was sort of tete de pont and a small picket of cavalry. The horse which led would not face the bridge, seeing the cavalry at the other end, but turned to one side, dashed into the stream and the whole 900 horses swam the river together.

"As they emerged and flew wildly on, the commander of the picket bethought him of a ruse and ordered the bugler to blow the appel. The old horses pricked up their ears, wavered, stopped, turned around and trotted back. This severed the mass—the whole 900 were recovered."

Foolish animals, you say—and yet human nature is little different. Many a sales force has stampeded for as ludicrous a cause. YOU are the commander of YOUR forces. Your men are watching you. Your frame of mind is their barometer. You can stampede them or you can steady them.

Take the lead. Keep up your own enthusiasm. Jump into the next three months with double determination. They will follow.

It's up to YOU.

Success and POWER

Napoleon Hill

Success and POWER are always found together. You cannot be sure of success unless you have power. You cannot have power unless you develop it through fifteen essential qualities.

Each of these fifteen qualities may be likened to the commanding officer of a regiment of soldiers. Develop these qualities in your own mind and you will have POWER.

The most important of the fifteen commanding officers in this army is DEFINITE PURPOSE.

Without the aid of a definite purpose the remainder of the army would be useless to you. Find out, as early in life as possible, what your major purpose in life shall be. Until you do this you are nothing but a drifter, subject to control by every stray wind of circumstance that blows in your direction.

Millions of people go through life without knowing what it is they want.

All have a purpose, but only two out of every hundred have a DEFINITE purpose. Before you decide whether your purpose is DEFINITE or not, look up the meaning of the word in the dictionary.

NOTHING IS IMPOSSIBLE TO THE PERSON WHO KNOWS WHAT IT IS HE WANTS AND MAKES UP HIS MIND TO ACQUIRE IT!

Source: *The Law of Success*. The Ralston University Press, 1928, Vol. VII, p. 137.

Courage is Mastery

George Harrison Phelps

Did you ever see a salesman tremble? Have you seen him mop his brow, his hands fidgeting nervously and his face the picture of a timid child?

There, standing right at the door of Opportunity, he wavered. FEAR overcame him. He is the salesman who feared only this morning that he would miss his car. He is the salesman who feared last night that he would lose his job; the one who feared his competitor would force him out, and was afraid that the other man's product would show up better than his own.

That salesman didn't start right. He never sold HIMSELF.

If he had, he wouldn't worry about his job. He would laugh at competition. He would forget the other fellow. He would march right into the Big Man's office and meet him as an equal. He would know no self-deprecation. Confidence in himself and confidence in his own car would take him anywhere. Confidence would talk for him. Confidence would Sell for him.

The last thing he'd do would be to fear the man whose needs he could supply.

Salesmanship today is a science. Mastery of science means study. Successful salesmanship means first of all successful study of oneself; secondly, successful study of the prospect. Fear will never facilitate study. Confidence will. It is the biggest asset of the man who leads.

Trembling is pre-historic—and so is selling. Both started away back in the dark ages when men craved stories in books of stone and savage mothers reared their broods in rock-hewn houses on mountain sides. In those days salesmen had a right to tremble. They did their dickering with rival tribes, armed with spears and eager for battle, lined up on every side behind trees and bushes. There was a middle ground between them and there the two salesmen deposited their wares, stealthily and one at a time. Each in turn sped out to see what the other had left. If the first felt the trade uneven he grunted, touched nothing, and returned. The other then dashed forth and added to his offering. Again the first surveyed the pile, and satisfied, picked up his rival's wares and plunged back in zigzag fashion to where his companions were hidden behind the trees. That was his way of closing the deal. Nostrils distended and with hands clutching nervously at their weapons, the other tribesmen had looked on to see that he took nothing but his own. A hundred crouched forms were poised for instant attack.

That was in pre-historic days. That was before salesmanship became a science.

Now the struggle is just as tense, but instead of using a knotted club the salesman conquers by confidence, by tact, by courage.

Courage is Mastery!

Courage

Napoleon Hill

Courage, however, is that firmness of spirit, that moral backbone which, while fully appreciating the danger involved, nevertheless goes on with the undertaking. Bravery is physical; courage is mental and moral. You may be cold all over; your hands may tremble; your legs may quake; your knees be ready to give way—that is fear. If, nevertheless, you do forward; if, in spite of this physical defection you continue to lead your men against the enemy, you have courage. The physical manifestations of fear will pass away. You may never experience them but once.

Source: *The Law of Success*. The Ralston University Press, 1928, Vol. III, p. 113.

Doing the Impossible

Madeleine Kay

Bumblebees should not be able to fly.

According to all the laws of physics and aerodynamics, they are totally unsuited for flight. Their bodies are too big and bulky. They are not shaped properly for flight. And they don't have a big enough wing-span for their body weight and mass.

Nevertheless ... they fly. They don't know they're not supposed to be able to.

We can learn a lot from bees and other animals. They are not plagued by fears and doubts as most of us are—the can I or could I's, the hows, the what ifs, or the should I's. They just do it—whatever it is they want to do ... or are meant to do. They don't keep second-guessing their ability or the outcome. Instead, they trust their inner knowing.

We too have that inner knowing. And deep down inside each one of us, we know what we want to do ... and what we are capable of doing. We need to surrender to that knowing ... and to have faith in our abilities in the face of our fears and doubts.

Dr. Hill calls that courage. "Courage," he says, "is mastery." And courage or confidence, will lead you to success in whatever you want to do, be or have. Courage is the result of confidence, Hill tells us … and confidence comes from knowing yourself. When you know yourself, you can go into any situation fortified by who you are … and therefore, unplagued by what I call the hidden shoulds.

Since bumblebees don't know the laws of resistance of air, they don't know or tell themselves that they should not be able to fly … and probably therefore, wouldn't. And if we didn't listen to what others say, or react to what we see, feel or tell ourselves, then we too would be able to ignore or bypass or simply, not even be aware of, all those hidden shoulds—telling us what we should or shouldn't be able to, what we should or shouldn't be afraid of … or to try or to go for.

Hill tells us courage comes from confidence … and that confidence comes from, what I call serendipity. Serendipity is the faculty inside each and every one of us that lets us eliminate "the voice of should"—to draw upon and live from our authentic self.

Serendipity allows you to be aware and responsive, so you can go beyond appearances … and function from and act out of what you know, not what you see or hear or feel.

Serendipity is a faculty inside you that expects, experiences and attracts the best. And a quality of serendipity is that knowing that gives you the courage to liberate the potential inside you … to be all that you can be and do whatever you want to do.

What could you do if you were unaware of the "supposed" limitations placed on you?

How could you soar to new heights if you let go of fear, anxiety, worry and doubt … or just what other people have told you that you cannot do or is impossible?

You can do the impossible, the difficult, the improbable....

Remember ... Anything ... no, *Everything* is Possible! Courage is mastery when you live serendipitously!

I am Action

George Harrison Phelps

Merchants, salesmen! In the roar of Europe's cannon did you discern a voice? Has it stolen to your ears through the din of destruction and whispered to you the revelation of its identity? Have you heard it spoken:

"I am Action."

Have you paused to grasp the lesson of the cannon? Do you pause at any time to grasp a lesson?

Have you compared big guns and big salesmen? Have you pictured walls of stone and iron crumbling beneath the violence of the shells, and have you marveled at the force impelling them?

Gun experts know how far a gun will carry on a given charge of powder. To increase the range they increase the powder—up to the capacity of the gun.

It is about the same with salesmen. Most of us are capable of carrying much farther than we do—we only need a little more powder.

The powder that carries the salesman through the crowd, and makes him ring the bell with an order, is action.

He must first have the right frame of mind—the right desire—the right aim. But this is not enough. Some of the greatest failures in the world have been those of thinkers and dreamers who had the right frame of mind—the right desire, and, generally speaking, the right aim, yet who just couldn't act.

Look at the names of the men in your own business who have become famous in their chosen work—they are great because they harnessed action to plan and drove with purpose.

Success is the direct result of desire intensified to the point of action. A clearly defined ideal, backed by a big charge of powder, must precede every permanent success.

Wet powder won't do. This is the day of the man who really acts—whose powder has propulsion in it. There never has been a time since we of the present generation can remember when opportunity of intelligent initiative and action offered such quick and certain reward.

Selling goods has undergone a change in the last few years and the end is not yet. Yesterday's methods and reputations will not bring the desired results today. It is up to each of us to count the number of times that we have called on a prospect and found that he had bought from some other firm the afternoon before, when we felt down deep in our own minds that we had been guilty of inaction and could have secured the order if we had been on the job. Doesn't it hurt?

When a prospect comes into our place of business he generally is interested in the purchase of something. We doubtless use our best selling talk to intensify that interest and to create a desire to buy. The prospect seems nearly closed, but leaves the store without buying, and we sometimes do much loud talking about the order we are going to get in the morning. But somehow we are terribly busy the next morning, and the call is postponed until afternoon. Perhaps we get him then, but if we do, it is luck.

Did you ever stop to think, Brother Salesman, that every time we postpone a "follow-up" we are allowing a perfectly good desire to go roaming around the streets unsatisfied—a prey for the live salesman next door? Well, we are, and it's ten to one that the very salesman next door is the one that we have been roasting as a lucky dog that got his job on a bluff. No, he didn't—he got it because he was alive and had the ability to take advantage of our inaction and to intensify the desire of our prospect sufficiently to get the name on the dotted line.

There is a law that governs all this. It is this: Every idea or conclusion which enters the mind of a prospective buyer is accepted as true unless hindered by some contradictory argument. The salesman with action is the one who never allows a prospect to run around loose without a pretty good antiseptic for contradictory arguments.

Think out a plan for every day's work—let nothing interfere with calls that you know you should make—a little forethought and planning will save a whole lot of running around, and a little clear seeing will save a pile of looking. Let me give you an example of how this works out.

An automobile dealer in the East went out on the back porch one morning to bring in the milk bottles. He found them flirting with the morning paper. By the latter he noticed that Doctor Brown, the village doctor, in answering a midnight call, had been thrown from his buggy in an accident that resulted in the death of his horse.

Without waiting for breakfast, this dealer jumped into his demonstrating car, drove to the doctor's office, and offered the doctor the emergency service of car and driver, without cost. The car never came back, for the doctor, long proof against anti-buggy suggestions, realized the need, and the salesman supplied it.

The successful salesman in this age of competition must have the ability to act—to see what should be done—then to "do it quick," caring nothing for precedent or tradition. Did Edison, Marconi, Burbank, Peary, or any other leader in the world's work follow the path of dead men? No; they dreamed, desired, acted and won.

When your prospect list gets low and you can't possibly see a sale in sight, sit down and think. Work out something from your own brain. You'll be surprised at the mass of good ideas that you have stored away, if you will just take a little time to dig them out.

Every day in your own town something happens that leads to a possible purchaser. The live salesman is the man who has cultivated the habit of seeing opportunities—and the habit of acting. The only habit that ever kept a man in a rut is the habit of not thinking—and not acting.

The greatest psychologists of the day have proved that the average man uses but a small fraction—say a third to a tenth—of his inherent brain power. The rest lies idle. Why? Because original thought has not put it to work—and the original way of thinking—your personal way of thinking—is the only way that will carry you to real success in your business.

SELL THIS THOUGHT TO YOURSELF—THEN TRANSLATE IT INTO ACTION.

Absolute Control

Napoleon Hill

You have ABSOLUTE CONTROL over but one thing and that is your thoughts. This is the most significant and inspiring of all facts known to man! It reflects man's Divine nature. This Divine prerogative is the sole means by which you may control your own destiny. If you fail to control your own mind, you may be sure you will control nothing else.

If you must be careless with your possessions, let it be in connection with material things. *Your mind is your spiritual estate!* Protect and use it with the care to which Divine Royalty is entitled. You were given a WILL-POWER for this purpose.

Unfortunately, there is no legal protection against those who, either by design or ignorance, poison the minds of others by negative suggestion. This form of destruction should be punishable by heavy legal penalties, because it may and often does destroy one's chances of acquiring material things which are protected by law.

Source: *Think and Grow Rich.* The Ralston Society, 1937, pp. 367–368.

Call to Action

Gus Gates

Access to information is more widespread today than at any time in history. Walk into any library. Look beyond the books, the audios, the movies, and the support staff who assist in finding resources. Look to the information gateway provided at no cost to library patrons in the online section. Libraries recognize that information is updated constantly. Providing online resources extends the library's relevance as a source of information. For many, speed of access is the key to information's usefulness. Mobile devices are used to link to resources for business and personal information gathering or dissemination. Mobile devices enable people to remain connected with each other and with expanding information.

Information access enables a keen sense of life. However, an improved future requires more than improved information access.

Leaders develop a clear vision of what is to come. Dr. Napoleon Hill observed that Edison, Marconi, Burbank, and Peary each blazed their own paths directed by a Definite Purpose of their own adoption. They had the "ability to act—to see what should be done—then do it quick."

Borrowing from wisdom of Dr. Hill, I promote the DDAA Cycle: Dream, Desire, Act, Achieve.

- *Dream* what can be—Adopt a Definite Purpose and organize your knowledge of the things you want.
- *Desire* a new reality—Build the Enthusiasm with-in to power you past adversity and defeats with-out.
- *Act* on a plan—Personal Initiative is the power that starts all action.
- *Achieve* a result—Celebrate Success & Learn from Adversity and Defeat.

Dr. Hill's concept of Personal Initiative is key to the progression of the DDAA Cycle. Personal Initiative is the character that drives a free society, for no person is free until he or she learns to do his or her own thinking and gains the courage to act on his or her own Personal Initiative. Remember, knowledge is NOT power. Knowledge-acted-upon is power.

When we organize our knowledge, and from that organization adopt a Definite Purpose, we begin the Dream. We must first conceive of something as a Dream before we act to cause it to come into being. (Can you cross a room without first envisioning yourself on the other side?)

The Dream becomes relevant when we develop a Desire for it to become reality. Building our Enthusiasm creates the Desire to sustain our actions when faced with adversity.

Dr. Hill compared a salesperson's action to the powder charge in a gun: The more powder in the gun, the more capacity for the shell to have an impact on the target. Similarly, when more action is taken in a salesperson's day, more capacity for sales results is created. Personal Initiative is the cause for Action—the powder in the gun.

Action will Achieve results—good or bad. Good results should be celebrated for they bolster the Dream. Even bad results provide an opportunity to learn from temporary defeat. Our results provide the new knowledge needed to gain a clearer vision of our Dream, a greater Desire for its becoming reality, and greater Personal Initiative to power our Actions and Achieve new results.

Take Action—Take Leadership.

Out of the Gloom

George Harrison Phelps

One evening a young man sat by the fire staring moodily at the blaze. He was discouraged, and life with its struggle for happiness seemed hardly worthwhile. Everything had gone wrong. From early youth people and circumstances had treated him shabbily. Lines of mistrust and melancholy had already begun to mark his forehead. His shoulders no longer squared themselves as he planned his work for the morrow. The old thrill of his profession had long since ceased to abide with him, and he felt that he was getting old. He was sure of it, because lately his health had been bothering him.

Just a few moments before his wife had chided him for his irritability. This, more than all else, contributed to the mood he was in, for she had always been the one cheerful and encouraging influence that had kept him plugging. And now the one person most important to his happiness had gone back on him. There was nothing left. He had lost his faith in humanity, if indeed he ever had any.

As he started for his office the next morning he determined to wind up his affairs with the greatest possible dispatch and enlist in the most hazardous branch of the service. He would use what little influencc he had to get himself immediate transportation to France.

As he bought his morning paper from the ragged little urchin on the station platform, he noticed that the youngster was tightly holding the hand of another little midget. Doubtless a sister. Scantily clad and shivering from the damp morning air, the urchin was contentedly munching an apple. Every now and then he would put his arm around the sister and hold the apple so that she could take a bite.

As he seated himself in his accustomed seat in the smoker he saw a young mother tenderly carrying a tiny white coffin on through to the baggage car. A young man across the aisle quickly jumped to her side and relieved her of her precious burden with a word or two of sympathy.

In the elevator, as he was being whisked to the floor on which he had his office, he met a chap who had just returned from a western city where he had gone to help some pal out of a nasty scrape. His office door was locked and after he had let himself in he found a note on his secretary's desk, telling him that she had gone to the pest house to spend the last hours with a girl who was slowly dying with a disease that one mentions only with a shudder.

His usual luncheon place was an exclusive restaurant in the business district where quietness was advertised as a special feature. The waitresses were fined if a dish was broken or anything occurred to mar the quietness of the place. At the next table a timid young girl spilled a few drops of coffee, and in her confusion collided with another waitress to the complete destruction of several dishes. After his meal was finished, the man at the next table hurriedly thrust a bill in the hand of the timid little girl and rushed for the elevator as though he had suddenly forgotten an important engagement.

When he reached the street our man saw a fellow club member tenderly leading his drunken son to a taxicab and people were gaping at him and knew him, for he was prominent in the city's affairs.

On the way back to his office he saw a young clerk rush frantically after a car and hand the conductor the nickel that had been overlooked, and in an alley nearby an old man was patiently trying to free a mongrel cur from his burden of tin.

That evening as he walked slowly toward his home our man thought of all these people he had seen and of the little kindnesses, and then he thought of himself and knew that the world was a gloomy place to live in because he had made it so. He understood now that to find real contentment and happiness and good-will one must think of other things besides one's self. He noticed, too, that he walked with a springier step and the evening twilight seemed particularly beautiful.

He saw his wife waiting for him at the door of their home and they passed on into the house with their arms about each other.

The Greek Wheel Of Fortune

Napoleon Hill

> *I am reminded, O king, and take this lesson to heart, that there is a wheel on which the affairs of men revolve and its mechanism is such that it prevents any man from being always fortunate. – Croesus*

What a wonderful lesson is wrapped up in these words of Croesus; a lesson of hope and courage and promise.

Who of us has not seen off days, when everything seemed to go wrong? These are the days when we see only the flat side of the great wheel of life.

Let us not forget that the wheel is always turning. If it brings us sorrow today, it will bring us joy tomorrow. Life is a cycle of varying events—fortunes and misfortunes.

We cannot stop this wheel from turning, but, we can modify the misfortune it brings us by remembering that good fortune will follow, just as day follows night.

> *To thine own self be true and it must follow, as the night the day, that thou canst not then be false to any man.*

Source: *Napoleon Hill's Magazine*. July, 1921, inside front cover.

The Little Old Lady

George Harrison Phelps

Have you ever had some stranger grasp your hand with a welcome smile that seemed to say, "I like you and want to know you better?" Do you remember how you felt—how, perhaps, you said the same thing to yourself, "I like YOU and want to know YOU better?" And afterwards when you met this same person again, how glad you were to see him?

We all meet people like that, and they are usually the ones with whom we like to associate. They become our friends; they get our business when we have it to give. They have our confidence and they prosper, for they are dispensing sunshine and good-will and happiness—commodities that are always in demand. In these days of busy business the supply seems limited and we haven't the time to waste with those who have none to offer. It is natural for us to spend our money with the salesman who is friendly. We go out of our way to trade where we are known, where a welcome smile greets us and the salesman calls our name.

Henry Ward Beecher says, "Nothing on earth can smile but man! Gems may flash reflected light, but what is a diamond-flash compared to an eye-flash and a mirth-flash? Flowers cannot smile; this is a charm that even they cannot claim. It is the prerogative of man; it is the color which love wears, and cheerfulness and joy—these three. It is a light in the windows of a face, by which the heart signifies it is at home and waiting. A FACE THAT

CANNOT SMILE IS LIKE A BUD THAT CANNOT BLOSSOM, AND DRIES UP ON THE STALK."

If we give friendship, we get friendship in return. If we are courteous, our customers are more likely to treat us in the same manner. Courtesy and good nature make it easy to buy. The indifferent salesman is a lodestone around the neck of any business. Friendliness has its own reward. It may not be apparent today, but it piles up for itself a wealth of interest that is negotiable in every industry. We never know at what moment it may mean the turning point in our business lives.

On a gloomy morning a few years ago a little old lady entered one of New York's great department stores. She was wet and disheveled and seemed to wander aimlessly about as though she were looking for nothing in particular. It was early and the clerks had not settled down to work. They were gathered in groups about the store, noisily discussing their personal affairs. No one paid the slightest attention to the little old lady until a young clerk noticed her aimless wandering and hurried to her side.

"What can I show you, Madam?" he asked. With an apology for the delay in waiting upon her he quickly secured the article she required and explained its merits courteously and thoroughly. After the purchase was made he left his counter and escorted her to the door, where he assisted her with her umbrella and the bundles she carried. Before she left the woman asked for his card.

A few days later this store received a letter from a woman ordering the complete furnishings for a great estate in Scotland. "In addition to this order," she wrote, "I want you to send your Mr. P——— to personally supervise the installation of these furnishings." The man she designated was the young clerk who had treated her so courteously that rainy morning.

"But, Madam," said the store manager later on, "this young man is one of our most inexperienced clerks and in no way fitted to carry out such an important mission. Let me suggest that we send our Mr. S———, who is one of the best interior decorators in the country."

"I am sorry," said the woman, "but I wish to have this young gentleman sail at once for Scotland and take immediate charge of the work!" And so this youngster, who knew the value of courtesy and a smile, crossed the Atlantic to direct the furnishing of one of the world's famous palaces.

THE LITTLE OLD LADY WAS MRS. ANDREW CARNEGIE.

Pleasing Personality

Napoleon Hill

Let us now summarize the chief factors which enter into the development of an attractive personality, as follows:

First: Form the habit of interesting yourself in other people; and make it your business to find their good qualities and speak of them in terms of praise.

Second: Develop the ability to speak with force and conviction, both in your ordinary conversational tones and before public gatherings, where you must use more volume.

Third: Clothe yourself in a style that is becoming to your physical build and the work in which you are engaged.

Fourth: Develop a positive character, through the aid of the formula outlined in this lesson.

Fifth: Learn how to shake hands so that you express warmth of feeling and enthusiasm through this form of greeting.

Sixth: Attract other people to you by first "attracting yourself" to them.

Seventh: Remember that your only limitation, within reason, is the one which YOU set up in YOUR OWN mind.

These seven points cover the most important factors that enter into the development of an attractive personality, but it seems hardly necessary to suggest that such a personality will not develop of its own accord. It will develop, if you submit yourself to the discipline herein described, with a firm determination to transform yourself into the person that you would like to be.

Source: *The Law of Success.* The Ralston University Press, 1928, Vol. VI, pp. 51, 53.

The Little Old Lady In All Of Us

Dr. Judy Arcy

When we were children we all heard the saying, "a smile is just a frown turned upside down." We also were taught that it takes fewer muscles to smile than frown. Both are good reasons for smiling, but is there a deeper reason for smiling? Napoleon Hill quoted Henry Ward Beecher as saying, "Nothing on earth can smile, but man.... It is the colors that love wears and is the light in the window of a face by which the heart signifies it is at home waiting." Most of us learned to smile as infants because it provided a pleasant response from our parents and caregivers. Dr. Hill goes even farther in his story of the Little Old Lady to exemplify the use of smiles, good manners and a generally pleasant disposition as tools for success.

The little old lady didn't display any of the common characteristics of a potential high level client. One of the clerks provided assistance to her and went the extra mile by explaining the merits of each product and escorting her to the door after she made her purchase. A few days later that clerk was given the opportunity of a lifetime, by that little old lady, even though he was one of the least experienced workers in the store. That little old lady was Mrs. Andrew Carnegie. One can speculate that he learned his good manners, pleasant nature and ability to treat people respectfully from his own experiences at home, in school and by social interactions.

We are taught basic manners at an early age. Simple responses of please, thank you, and you are welcome are verbal smiles. In today's busy, technologically sophisticated world, we often forget the niceties. It appears that at times decorum is even lacking among celebrities, politicians, and our social leaders. Our ability to communicate rapidly via Internet, text and telephone has fostered the development of a new vernacular, abbreviated spelling and deletion of "unnecessary" words and/or letters. Do we need to eliminate the polite demeanor or can it be retained in our fast paced world as part of speedy communication?

Manners for success are a two-way street. One must be open to accepting help and kindness with a friendly attitude as well as providing the help. Dr. Hill urges us to invest in our own future with courtesy, smiles and good manners. By graciously accepting kindness you are better able to pass it along and become more comfortable with manners and with people. People are most likely to do business or trade with someone with whom they feel comfortable, respected and relaxed. A knowledgeable, pleasant interaction with clients is more likely to facilitate a more successful business life.

Dr. Hill's words about smiles and manners are still appropriate today. The value of a smile for both the giver and the receiver can be priceless. A popular soft drink commercial shows a man picking up a dropped object and returning it to the owner—who then opens a door for another person, smiling—who in turn helps someone across the street. This is a graphic of how going the extra mile can change the world.

Feminine Salesmanship

George Harrison Phelps

There are two ways of catching the wily woodchuck. You can go after him with a lasso and a club. You might land him. You can lay low, find his trail, put a very tempting bait above two steel jaws on a hair trigger, and play the waiting game. You've got him this way every time.

There are two ways of selling a prospect: going after him with a club, and playing the subtler game; giving him a chance to persuade himself. It is a far cry from the haggling market places of the East to the modern marts of commerce. The philosophy of business and the ideals of salesmanship have evolved a lot since those days. Now confidence is the keynote of the sale. The buyer must have absolute satisfaction.

As we become more civilized, more enlightened, we give up the crude, the aggressive method of attack. We study the simple psychology of the individual, or, if you want to get rid of the word psychology, we get closely acquainted with the man and his method of reaching decisions. We appeal to the buyer's desires and impulses. We compel him to decide as we will, because we sell a logical proposition and we arrange our logic so that it rams itself home. We just sit by to be sure that our logic has a straight track.

We are abandoning more and more the masculine, the argumentative, the dictatorial type of salesmanship. I sometimes think that a good way of describing it is to say that we are rapidly developing feminine salesmanship. I use the term feminine advisedly, for the feminine element is creative, the masculine destructive. Napoleon was a perfect masculine type. He sowed a whirlwind of shell and fire and reaped a harvest of slaughter and death. He died in exile far from his beloved France.

Pericles was tyrant at Athens during the most glorious period of Greek history. He was a builder, a creator, an artist; an idealist who made real his dreams in the marble temples of the Acropolis. He got all his good ideas from a woman, Aspasia. She was the dominating power in this golden age of Greece. She had her way without armour or fanfare or flag. She was one of the great forerunners of feminine salesmanship. She signed Pericles up for the greatest city of all time.

The approach is the most important feature of the sale. It makes no difference what the worth of your article or the real need which it fills, if you can't get a prospect's attention and interest. You may have the surest selling-talk in the business. If you cannot get it across, you may as well forget it and start raising ginseng. Professor Bojack, of Bojack's Correspondence School, suggests that you either do a quick sprint to Friend Prospect's desk, or take off your shoes and sneak up quietly on your hands and knees, or blow up the stretch on a motorcycle. These three ways of approach are a trifle exaggerated. Yet they contain an underlying truth. The approach must be made calmly, subtly, adroitly—meaning by these abused words simply an approach sensitive to all conditions. The problem consists in reaching the prospect's reason and understanding on a sympathetic basis from his point of view, and getting him to sell himself to your way of thinking. Right here we may learn from the ladies. There was Cleopatra, for example, the sorceress of the Nile.

Egypt was in a state of civil war. The land was divided between the forces of Ptolemy and the forces of Cleopatra. Caesar happened along and, sending his invincible Tenth Legion into the city demanded immediate surrender to Rome.

Ptolemy's men stacked arms. Cleopatra's resisted and were driven beyond the borders. Caesar took charge of the royal palace.

Cleopatra wanted an interview with Caesar that she might present her cause. She knew she had an unanswerable argument. She sent him a night-letter—"I am Cleopatra, Queen of Egypt, and I would speak with you."

There was no reply to her request, however. It was a common thing to find many pretenders to a throne. He would make Egypt a Roman province and have an end to the matter.

Caesar was used to settling questions with the sword. But now he was dealing with a woman.

In the retinue of Cleopatra was a giant Numidian slave, his tongue torn out as a sign that he should tell no royal secrets. Just at dusk a centurion on guard at the palace gates came to Caesar in the study where he was busy dictating the "Commentaries" of different campaigns to four ram-lamb stenogs at once.

"A slave is at the portal, bearing a rich and finely woven rug, the gift of a noble of Alexandria to the Imperial Caesar."

"Yes, yes; tell him to leave it and bear my thanks to his master."

"But he insists on presenting it in person."

"Well, have him come in."

Enter a gigantic, swarthy slave, a great rug upon his ebony shoulder. He places his burden gently on the floor, undoes the silken cord, and out of the center of the roll steps—Cleopatra.

"I am Cleopatra, Queen of Egypt."

"Yes, yes, my child."

"I am Cleopatra and I would speak with you alone."

Caesar waves centurions and secretaries from the room. They are alone and Cleopatra has conquered by her indirect method.

Did Cleopatra give up the game when Caesar ignored her? Did she say, "It can't be done?" No. She found a way to get Caesar's order. She did not meet him on the march and argue the question with him. She used suggestion. She took no chances on argument. She was instinctively putting into play the principle of feminine salesmanship.

This principle revolves around the feminine method of attack and control; suggestion and inference rather than argument. The superiority of the feminine, the suggestive, method lies in the fact that unquestioning action follows at once upon the giving of the suggestion, while the result of presenting arguments is deliberation with the attendant hesitation.

Walter Dill Scott, director of the Psychological Laboratory at Northwestern University, says that mankind is influenced more by suggestions than by syllogistic arguments. As a practical salesman I subscribe to his argument. It all reminds us of that old song, "Her lips were so near that—what else could I do?" The identity of live advertising and salesmanship with Woman's persuasive way is quite obvious. Professor Scott is unconsciously arguing for Feminine Salesmanship.

I rather think that the world of business is just waking to the value of feminine salesmanship; a practical working method, used by women from the time Eve persuaded Adam to take the first bite, down through Cleopatra, who conquered two emperors of Rome; Aspasia, who inspired Pericles to create "the glory that was Greece"; Theodora, who compiled the Roman Law Code, with the aid of Justinian, and had the last word in its arrangement; Isabella, who enabled Columbus to discover the New World; Martha Washington, who was behind George, even at Valley Forge, up to and including the tango-danseuse of today. The subtle, suggestive, persuasive way wins. Also it makes alluring sales copy and sure selling methods.

Here is the real force behind successful advertising and selling. Let us realize this power of feminine salesmanship. Consciously and scientifically, let us employ it in making our advertising efficient, our sales effective. It is better than the hypnotic notion of selling which some people have—the notion that you can "sing 'em to sleep" and get them to sign up in a trance. That is poor salesmanship. The big way is woman's old-fashioned way of getting man to do what she wants while he's thinking the thing is his own plan and decision!

Her Mental Attitude

Napoleon Hill

The determining factor as to the use a woman makes of her sex emotion—whether she uses it as a stimulant with which to inspire the man of her choice to aim high and work hard to attain his goal, or merely permits it to be spent in physical expression—is her own mental attitude. If a woman's mental attitude is not one of harmony, cooperation, enthusiasm, initiative and self-control it is almost certain that her entire influence upon the man of her choice will be wholly or partly detrimental to him. The subject of mental attitude has been analyzed in another chapter, but I wish to here emphasize its importance, because it is the factor which determines whether one's sex emotion serves as a help or a hindrance in attaining the material needs of life and the spiritual joy of happiness.

No woman can be of help to the man of her choice, and no woman can long influence or hold her man, unless her mental attitude toward him, and in connection with every other human relationship, is harmonious, cooperative and sympathetic. A bad disposition simply converts the sex emotion into a power of destruction that can end only in misery, poverty and the things of Life one does not want; and it may as well be said here and now that every woman who is suffering the inconvenience of poverty and unhappiness can find the cause by examining her mental attitude toward other people. Every woman who gains the love of a man and then loses it can trace the loss directly to a change in her own mental attitude, no matter how many alibis or "other women" she may create to explain away her loss. Let us face the facts and admit that both our failures and our successes, in every human relationship (and especially in relationship between men and women where sex is involved) are due to our personal habits which establish our mental attitude.

Men who rise to great heights of success in business, and then go down in permanent defeat, can trace their failure to nothing except a change in their mental attitude. In this truth woman may find her greatest asset, which is her ability to transmute her sex emotion into practical forms of inspiration with which she helps the man of her choice to stage a comeback after defeat. Seldom is a man so broken through defeat that the woman of his choice cannot give him new courage and a new start in life, if only she will condition her mental attitude so it is at all times inspiring.

Source: *How to Attract Men and Money*, by Napoleon and Rosa Lee Hill. The Napoleon Hill Foundation, 2012, pp. 47–48.

The Gift

Adora Spencer

As I sit on a camel at the foot of the enormous Sphinx and the Pyramids it guards, I am keenly aware of the power and magnitude of masculine energy. Cleopatra's delicate curves must have been a wonderful contrast to this desert. Her presence, I imagine, was a gift to this place and Egypt was a gift to her. As I have now lived among the Egyptian women for almost two months, I can see the power of feminine salesmanship highly at work here, even today.

Noha Wagih is a great example of someone who uses Feminine Salesmanship rather than force. She is lovely and feminine. She is powerful and bright. Her bio alone shows the results she has already claimed—Author, TV presenter, Marketing Director for a major Egyptian movie studio, etc. A few days ago I got to witness her in action. The men were in the other room debating over a business decision. She sat, relaxed in her chair, head back. I asked, "Noha, I wonder what they are saying?" She replied, "Adora, it doesn't matter. They are going to come out and tell us anyway. Then they will ask us what we think and we will do what we want, no matter what happened in that room."

I was on edge, anticipating their decision. Finally they entered the room we were waiting in. It was astounding. They told us, "We have decided that Adora will leave now and come back later. It is the holiday season and things are too busy. Make sense?"

Noha took a deep, relaxed breathe and sat straight up. "Media never sleeps, even during the holidays. We all know that. Now is the best time for her to be here, preparing for January … when everyone starts working again."

The spokesperson replied, "Yes, you are right. It's done. Adora, you are our guest as long as you would like to be here. Welcome to the team. Can we go now?"

What?! After hours of debating and making up their minds in one moment it was all turned around? Later I spoke with Noha. She explained. "Adora, you have to let them have their talks. Let them argue it out. There is no need to be involved in that. Then when they come to you gently suggest your opinion only after they have asked for it."

Noha's gentle but powerful way of being makes them continuously ask for her advice. It is an inspiration to watch.

In my opinion, Pleasing Personality is the same as Feminine Salesmanship. It is the lighter way to get things done. It is taking time to be courteous, to listen and to understand the person you are dealing with. Then it is about learning to communicate what you want to that person in a way that occurs as an opportunity to them and honors them. When you can do that, you can accomplish almost anything you want. When it comes down to it, we all want the same basic things and everything else is just the details of how we get those things. If we know we are going to get what we want—love, peace, power, fulfillment, the opportunity to make a difference or whatever it is we are seeking—we will usually comply. Most people just spend too much time pushing the "details" instead of investigating and nurturing the core values in the people they are trying to collaborate with.

Cleopatra, Napoleon Hill and all those he interviewed knew this secret. You know this secret. What will you do with it? How will you use it?

Here are a few suggestions.

Instead of selling your idea, think collaboration. When you think collaboration you naturally think of your side and their side of things. This is different than, "I have something that I want you to buy." Collaboration is about two parties working together to get what they want. How can you help the other party get what they want and get what you are after at the same time?

Listen, listen, listen and listen some more. What are the people in your life really saying to you? What are their passions? What is motivating them, truly? Do you know? When they are talking, when do their eyes light up? When you notice their eyes light up ask them more questions around that topic. You will learn a LOT.

Then, think creatively. How can you help them experience more of what they are passionate about through their collaboration with you?

If you apply these suggestions you may begin to notice that people want to be around you more. They want to work with you, because you have taken the time to know them and to value them. Working with you will occur as an opportunity for them to experience more of what they love in their lives. What a gift? That is the power of developing a more Pleasing Personality. You get what you want through giving people more of what they want. That is the gift of Feminine Salesmanship.

Procrastinators

George Harrison Phelps

I sat in the reception room near a Big Man's office. I could look through the glass partitions and see him slowly opening his morning mail. He seemed to have other things on his mind besides the letters he was handling, and yet he went through the motions of opening, sorting and distributing to the various baskets as though his mind was concentrated perfectly upon the task.

Just then he sent for me, motioned me to a chair beside his desk and continued to open his mail. I watched him carefully, for I am interested in the methods of big men. Every now and then I could see that he came upon a letter that made him frown. Such letters he would place in a little pile over near his dictaphone. The remainder he kept in his hand and with a few words of apology proceeded to answer them. Rapidly and without hesitation he finished the pile and turned to me with a sigh of relief.

"What about that other pile?" I asked, indicating the letters that had caused the frowns. "Oh, that," he said, "why that's a bunch of complaints I'll have to tackle later on. I don't feel just like it right now. Somehow I always hate to start the morning answering complaints. It puts me in bad humor."

Just what I thought. He was putting off until later the disagreeable tasks. This big business man wasn't a bit different than you or I or a million other inefficient people who won't admit to themselves that they are procrastinators who take the lines of least resistance. We do though, in almost everything we tackle. We will mow the entire lawn and save that little tuft over by the rose bushes until the last just because it is hard to get at. We let that broken pane in the cellar window stay unrepaired, knowing full well the mice will get into the house and raise the dickens. And so on indefinitely. Fishes seem to be about the only things that are willing to tackle the hard jobs in preference to the easy ones. Fishes, you know, usually swim upstream.

Once there was a king who noticed that the road to his palace, down back of the postern gate, was being divided by the traffic that daily passed that way. It seems there was a rock in the middle of the road. Not a large rock, but just a medium size one that could easily have been removed, had someone been willing to spend an hour at the task. But no one did and the rock stayed there and all the wayfarers went around it, making a new bit of road.

The king, who was a very wise old king and loved his subjects and wished to make them happier, decided to teach them a lesson.

One night after dark he sent a mason to the place where the road was divided with instructions to chisel a small hole in the underside of the rock. In this hole the king placed a beautiful gold casket, and inside the casket a wonderful jewel of fabulous worth. Soon after, a neighboring kingdom declared war upon our king and the jewel casket was forgotten. But the people still traveled daily by the postern gate and around the rock. No one bothered to roll it out of the way. Years went on and one day the king fell very ill and knew that he was going to die. He called his courtiers to him and requested that after his death, the funeral procession pass by the postern gate, but not around the rock. He instructed that the most deserving of his retainers was to roll the rock out of the way, and for the years of faithful service was to receive whatever might be found there.

And so while the great funeral procession halted, the old retainer lifted the rock and revealed the casket and the priceless jewel to all the king's subjects. "If only I had rolled the stone aside," they all thought to themselves.

There are many stones along the road of life. Jewels are buried under most of them. It is easier to pass around—and quicker. But the journey's end finds us still out of purse.

If you would travel wisely, clear the road ahead. Don't avoid the rocks.

Roll them away!

Sustained Effort

Napoleon Hill

Industriousness is the capacity for sustained effort.

Imagination may dream the new thing and initiative may start this new thing, but it takes INDUSTRIOUSNESS to keep it going to success. The power of continued effort which, day in and day out, tirelessly and unceasingly holds a man always on the track of his objective is industriousness. The industrious man is always on the job. No opportunity may present itself too early in the morning for him to seize with ready hand. No evening has too late an hour for him to do business in. He watches no clock; and his hours of effort are not limited. He prosecutes his business both day and night.

Inertia is the way of dead things. They naturally do not move. There is a constant temptations to shirk your work or duty. To the extent that you yield to it you are a dead one. Why do more than you have to? Why not watch the boss, the clock, the partner, the client, the parishioner, and others for whom we work? Very well. Do so. Nemesis is right around the corner, and the law of averages will soon get you fired. Take your choice.

Source: *Napoleon Hill's Magazine*. April, 1923, p. 28.

Get Away With the Gun

George Harrison Phelps

When I was in school, there was a man on the track team by the name of Jimmy Dreyfus. He never really amounted to much and some of us used to wonder how he kept his place there. We knew he never was permitted to accompany the team on any of its travels, and it was a foregone conclusion that he would never compete in a championship meet. Jimmy just couldn't seem to make good. He tried hard enough, the Lord knows. He never "broke" training and he really worked like the dickens, but his "time" was always about a second too slow.

It began to look as though Jimmy's chance of winning his letter was gone beyond all hope. Then one day something happened. It was during an intercollegiate meet and we were fighting for every point we could get. We needed all three points in the "hundred" if we were to win the pennant. Our best short distance man was just finishing the low hurdles, when I heard the crowd's quick intake of breath which always means "something has happened," and in a moment our only sure winner was being carried off the track with a broken ankle.

Our side of the grand stand simply groaned with misery. All hope was gone. We had no one to take his place. Victory was being literally snatched from our grasp. Then suddenly, Mike, our old trainer, came trotting out from the club house with Jimmy Dreyfus following close behind. Ridiculous! Why humiliate us further? "Jimmy Dreyfus has no more chance of winning the hundred yard dash than a snail," we thought. And yet there he was, peeling off his bathrobe and limbering up for his first heat. "Mike must have gone crazy!" The audience was so taken by surprise that a hush had fallen over both grand stands. Everyone could hear him as he said to Jimmy, "Now listen here, Kid, you've got to save the day. I've been saving you for just such an occasion as this. You're the fastest man for short distances that ever trod a cinder track, but you've never been able to get away with the gun. Today you're going to do it, for I'm going to be right here to make you." And then we saw Mike slowly pull a raw-hide quirt from his hip pocket. Jimmy was on the mark and the starter began to count. Mike raised the quirt over his head. The pistol and Mike's whip seemed to crack at the same time.

And then the crowd went wild. Jimmy seemed to have beaten the gun and was running like a wild man down the stretch.

The spectators with a mighty shout swarmed over the stands onto the track. It was all over. Jimmy was being carried off the field as the announcer bawled through his megaphone, "One hundred yard dash won by Jimmy Dreyfus. Time, nine and four-fifths seconds, equaling the world's amateur record."

A few months ago, or on November eleventh to be exact, the sound of another kind of starting gun reverberated around the world. It was the signal for the beginning of a new race—a race in which we all compete. It meant, too, the turning of a new leaf; the rejuvenating of our forces for bigger things to come. Some have been slow to limber up. Now and then we find someone who failed to get on the mark. He is being left at the post while his rival merchants are running on in record time.

The race is still on. Every day sees the beginning of a new heat. Take a lesson from Jimmy Dreyfus and get away with the gun.

The Law of Compensation

Napoleon Hill

> *Take what figure you will, its exact value, no more nor less, still returns to you. –Emerson*

Time brings us mighty evidences of the existence of the Law of Compensation. Justice is never defeated; it is often postponed.

A true perspective of the Law of Compensation can only be gained by considering time and space. Rewards for virtue and punishment for wrong doing are often withheld for years and even from one generation to another.

Generally, however, the Law of Compensation works with comparative swiftness. "Crime and punishment grow out of one stem." By and large we reap that which we sow. A man may be a cheat and a fraud and seem to be getting away with the fruits of his stealthy practices, but there comes a time when he pays dearly through the loss of confidence and the withholding of friendliness by neighbors.

On the other hand, a man may practice the Golden Rule for a long period of time and still seem to fail to reap the fruits of his ethical conduct, but who can say how much he will be paid in happiness which he would not have enjoyed but for this practice. It is the exception and not the rule when the world neglects or willfully withholds pay that corresponds to the quality and quantity of the service a man renders it. The Law of Compensation often works quietly and unnoticed except by the person who is attuned to hear its silent message. The wise man neither doubts the existence of nor pranks with the Law of Compensation. He makes his conduct conform to its nature, thereby harnessing it to his purpose in life.

Source: *Napoleon Hill's Magazine*. March, 1922, p. 44.

Get Away With the Gun

LuAn Mitchell

Dr. Napoleon Hill accurately said, "Your great benefit may be where you are now."

But, often we are short sighted, we respond with—oh no, not me. I'm the hard done by, I am the victim, I am the forgotten. The story of Jimmy and his tenacity and courage reminds us that we are right now exactly where our very own greatest benefit may lie!

That "something" that binds us can be the very same "something" that frees us! How exciting, how wonderful, and how very good! We have so much to be grateful for, even those things that look like burdens or curses.

Dr. Hill reminds us that the best way to sell ourselves to others is to first sell the others to ourselves. But they are judgmental, they are mean to me, and to add to the mix they are bigots, how can I buy into their evil, and why would I want to? you may ask. Well let's use the fine example in "Get Away with the Gun" as an illustration of how Jimmy was given a chance, the stadium scowled and cringed when he seemed to have beaten the gun and ran like a "wild man" down the stretch. Then the energy shifted as Jimmy tied the world's amateur record!

Yes his great benefit was right there where he was, all along, but who would have guessed it? Jimmy kept the faith, he stayed the course he made the day!

The whole world is undergoing "renovations" of a sort, indeed we are "in a way, under construction." We are rethinking and reevaluating what we used to take for granted to be impossible, or undesirable, just like Jimmy being placed in the race in the

11th hour, yet he was the obvious choice, the perfect choice, the "missing link!" The hero and the humble young man who never stopped believing he was prepared at any given moment to receive his great benefit right where he was, and with that attitude and faith in a "bigger picture" he did the work and he trained hard and he waited for the call. Yes, the unlikely candidate, the underdog our determined "outcast" Jimmy was in fact not an outcast at all, but was a hidden jewel, he was to become the great benefit and the great teacher to everyone else, when he saved the day, as well! How fantastic! We have a lot to learn from Dr. Hill's teachings and from the truth of every situation, we can learn to see beyond what we are mistakenly told sometimes, and we can overcome and rise above, at anytime, anywhere.

Dr. Hill said, "Before success comes in any man's life he's sure to meet with much temporary defeat and perhaps some failures. When defeat overtakes a man, the easiest and most logical thing to do is quit. That is exactly what the majority of men do."

But not our Jimmy, and not MIKE THE TRAINER, he believed in Jimmy. He saw something more when he imparted to Jimmy, "Now look kid, you have to save the day, I have been saving you for just such an occasion as this!" The least likely candidate, why would a coach say he was saving a "dud" for an occasion such as this? He said it because as Dr. Hill tells us he knew Jimmy had it in him, he knew not to judge by appearances, he knew in his heart that Jimmy's time had come!

Dr. Hill's words have resonated with me many times in my life as well, when he said, "Every adversity, every failure, every heartache carries with it the seed of an equal or greater benefit."

Yes, it is true, I also met a great teacher and a great mentor of mine after a great tragedy in my life. It was after the death of a fine husband and the father of my children, I thought nothing could ever lift the veil of pain I was crushed beneath. His name was Charlie Tremendous Jones. Mr. Jones reminded me a lot of Dr. Napoleon Hill whom I was very familiar with because my mother had given me Dr. Hill's books to read when I was a child. Charlie "T" told me he was "hugging me with his heart" after he read my painful recounts in my book, *Leadership Lessons Learned by the Impossible Dreamer*. It was just that kind of hug across the miles, that helped a single mother struggling with financial and corporate pit falls, a hug that helped me through many sleepless confused nights filled with tears and fears. I was called to smile for the cameras so to speak, to put on a happy face, and "run the race," day in and day out as a mother with small children many people (thoughtfully saw me work very hard to make ends meet and survive my grief) but publically and privately banked on my failure.

But not Charlie Tremendous Jones, no, he saw something different than the others saw. Mr. Jones' voice still rings in my ears right alongside Dr. Napoleon Hill's wise messages, and coach Mike's belief in Jimmy. Yes, even when well-wishers thought my life was on a downward spiral I saw the light of a new day because I wanted to train hard for the moment I would be called in for my team.

Now there is a new generation, of runners, my own children who are young adults who have all been brought up on the wisdom of this "new day in the morning teaching."

We may be "under construction,". and it may get a little "dusty" from time to time, while we are renovating and updating old limiting beliefs for the new picture unfolding, but please make no mistake ... we DO have a perfect blueprint, and we have the right and perfect location for a bright new day to begin for us all!

With great vision, from the wise words of Dr. Napoleon Hill, and great examples in inspiring stories like Jimmy and marvelous real life friends in our lives like the beautiful Charlie Tremendous Jones, it is an absolutely perfect place to be exactly right where we are, (no matter what it may appear to be) and YES the absolutely perfect time is right now, if we are alert and we are ready!

Dr. Hill wisely advised us that, "Desire is the starting point of all achievement, not a hope, not a wish, but a keen pulsating desire which transcends everything!"

The race is on, are you satisfied to be just a spectator, or a fast and faithful front runner?

It's up to us.

Use Your Heart

George Harrison Phelps

As I close my eyes and look back a few years—and not so very many years at that—I can still hear my dad, as he used to call me when I had found some particularly hard nut to crack. "Use your head, son—use your head! That's what you've got it for," he would say. Seems like someone has always been telling me to use my head, and even now my big, genial boss does frequently resort to the same command, clothing his phrases with certain colorful expostulations, according to my density at that particular moment.

"Use your head!" How often we have heard it said. And yet few of us stop to realize that HARD WORK IS THE THING THAT MAKES A SALESMAN OR A SUCCESS of any kind. It sometimes has the fancy name of INITIATIVE, but HEAD WORK it is in common every-day language.

Thomas Feeney, of Boston, tells the story of Sing Foo, who was dying at the Homeopathic Hospital, eight thousand miles from his home. He was alone in a strange country. Before he died he asked for his one friend in the city—another Chinaman from the town in which he was born. At five o'clock in the afternoon a hospital attendant telephoned the information operator at a local exchange, and asked Miss Martha Bithell to find Yee Ling—address unknown. The request was unusual. The call did not come from a wealthy home or a great business house—but from a lowly Chinese laundryman. Miss Bithell started to work without a moment's hesitation.

A Chinese restaurant was the first place called. Miss Bithell's questions were treated with characteristic Oriental indifference. She wasted no time, but tried a more prosperous Chinese store. The proprietor offered little encouragement except to suggest two or three other numbers that she might try. The minutes slipped by. The trail led Miss Bithell to places in Boston, Cambridge, Brookline, Brighton and Waltham. She talked with many Chinamen—but she was not discouraged—she was on the job to stay. Nearly two hours after the search began she located a Chinaman named Tom Lee, for whom Yee Ling worked. After considerable difficulty Yee Ling was persuaded to step to the 'phone—but the result was a failure. They could not make each other understand. Again Miss Bithell USED HER HEAD. She remembered a Chinaman with whom she had previously talked, whose attitude showed that he was willing to assist. She soon had him on the line, and he agreed to help her out of her predicament by acting as interpreter. And so the message from his dying friend was told to Yee Ling in his native tongue.

Sing Foo died a few days later, never knowing that his last hours had been made happy because a friendly little telephone operator had USED HER HEAD.

And so, Brother Salesmen, I give you the same message that my dad used to give to me—USE YOUR HEAD, SON—USE YOUR HEAD! THAT'S WHAT YOU'VE GOT IT FOR.

The Service You Render

Napoleon Hill

Your forefathers may have come over on the Mayflower; you may have been born in the aristocratic part of Old Virginia; you may be a graduate of Yale, Harvard, or Princeton, with a string of degrees after your name a yard long, and, you may know more than any person on the works, but, you will still have to face the unescapable fact that the world will pay you for only one thing and that is the SERVICE you actually render, which reminds me of a certain chap who looked foolish but spoke wisely when he said: "These fat Poland China Hawgs are all right for looks but an old razor-backed porker will root a damned-sight better living any day."

Source: *Napoleon Hill's Magazine.* March, 1922, inside back cover.

Keep On Tapping

George Harrison Phelps

One morning about thirty years ago, just as the dim outlines of Mount Diablo began to show through the fog of San Pablo bay, a group of prominent San Francisco business men rowed with muffled oars to an old anchored barge on which was to be staged one of the greatest prize fights in history. It was James J. Corbett's first professional appearance, and was destined to be the beginning of a new era in the world of sport. Only a young insurance clerk and absolutely unknown, Corbett was matched against Joe Choynski, already something of a veteran in the ring.

Just as dawn was breaking the two boys who had been rivals from childhood took their corners. Both had just passed twenty, and their physically perfect bodies shone like marble in the dim light as they threw off their overcoats and stepped up for the hand shake.

Choynski had the open, frank face of a youngster in his teens, with a muscular chest and arm development of a gladiator. Corbett, more of the lithe, agile type, was perfectly symmetrical, and as clean-limbed as a woman. They both gave the appearance of masterpieces in sculpture from some such hand as Rodin.

"Jim," said Billy Delaney, Corbett's trainer, just before the fight, "you've only one chance in a thousand of winning. Joe can knock you cold if he can reach you. Keep tapping at his head. Keep EVERLASTING tapping. Never let up as long as you've got a breath left. Watch your foot work and tap, tap, tap until you wear him out."

With infinite skill, the contestants spent the first three rounds in trying each other out. Not a blow was struck. And then Choynski started a terrific battering. The force behind his rushes was enough to fell a tree.

But Corbett side-stepped with the agility of a panther. And then he began—swift, lighting-like jabs that would snap Joe's head back like a catapult.

"First blood," murmured the spectators as a stream of crimson trickled down Choynski's face. Round after round Corbett kept up his fiendish tapping. Once in a clinch, he landed a blow on Choynski's head that sounded like the crack of a rifle. From then on Corbett fought only with his left for he had broken several bones in his hand.

Still the tapping continued. Choynski fought on, although his face was swollen to a hideous shape, and he was covered with blood from head to foot. He tried to work his features into something like a ghastly smile as he scorned his trainer's advice to quit. "Kill me first," he said.

At the beginning of the twenty-eighth round Joe was helpless and incapable of defense. Corbett was dapper and fresh and unmarked. As Choynski staggered to the center of the ring, Corbett slapped him with the flat of his hand. A child would have laughed at the blow, but the great, broad-chested Choynski slid to the floor to be counted out.

At that moment Gentleman Jim, as he was often called, started on his great career to the championship of the world. And to the very end he never forgot Bill Delaney's advice to "keep on tapping."

In nature, and business and sport, in everything, it's all the same. Mountains have been worn away by the incessant fall of water. Puny men have built great pyramids and with their frail hands have brought into being cities of fabulous size. But these were not the achievements of a single day. They tell of infinite patience and fortitude.

In our struggle for success we are all tempted at times to land a blow at some unexpected opening, but the surest way is Corbett's way—to stand our ground and KEEP ON TAPPING.

Definite Chief Aim

Napoleon Hill

Thus it will be seen that all who succeed work with some definite, outstanding aim as the object of their labors.

There is some one thing that you can do better than anyone else in the world could do it. Search until you find out what this particular line of endeavor is, make it the object of your definite chief aim and then organize all of your forces and attack it with the belief that you are going to win. In your search for the work for which you are best fitted, it will be well if you bear in mind the fact that you will most likely attain the greatest success by finding out what work you like best, for it is a well-known fact that a man generally best succeeds in the particular line of endeavor into which he can throw his whole heart and soul.

Let us go back, for the sake of clarity and emphasis, to the psychological principles upon which this lesson is founded, because it will mean a loss that you can ill afford if you fail to grasp the real reason for establishing a definite chief aim in your mind. These principles are as follows:

First: Every voluntary movement of the human body is caused, controlled and directed by thought, through the operation of the mind.

Second: The presence of any thought or idea in your consciousness tends to produce an associated feeling and to urge you to transform that feeling into appropriate muscular action that is in perfect harmony with the nature of the thought.

For example, if you think of winking your eyelid and there are no counter influences or thoughts in your mind at the time to arrest action, the motor nerve will carry your thought from the seat of government, in your brain, and appropriate or corresponding muscular action takes place immediately.

Stating this principle from another angle: You choose, for example, a definite purpose as your lifework and make up your mind that you will carry out that purpose. From the very moment that you make this choice, this purpose becomes the dominating thought in your consciousness, and you are constantly on the alert for facts, information and knowledge with which to achieve that purpose. From the time that you plant a definite purpose in your mind, your mind begins, both consciously and unconsciously, to gather and store away the material with which you are to accomplish that purpose.

Source: *The Law of Success.* The Ralston University Press, 1928, Vol. II, pp. 53–54.

Confidence

George Harrison Phelps

Salesmanship is just as scientific as any other profession and accordingly, should be given the same careful study that one naturally would give to the study of medicine, or law, or civil engineering, or the hundreds of other professions that require systematic training. Success in any line of effort comes through the operation of law. It doesn't very often come by chance or accident; at least nobody gets very far by waiting for that chance to come of its own accord.

In the working out of Nature's laws, there is no such thing as an accident. A piece of rock tumbles from the side of a mountain and lands in the way of a limited train. We are inclined to call this an accident, but it simply is the result of Nature's forces having acted on that rock for a few hundred years or so.

Just as it's true of Nature, so is it true of business, of salesmanship, of the professions, of your personal success and mine. Considering the fact that the success of most of us is measured by our ability to sell things, wouldn't it be a mighty good plan to make a study of the fundamental laws that govern our chosen work?

Across the façade of a New England court house is carved this phrase, "Obedience to Law is Liberty." That's a mighty good adage to carve on the front of a court house, and I don't think it would work much harm to the salesman who pasted it in the front of his hat.

Let us consider for a moment the first and really great law of successful salesmanship, in fact one of the great laws of success in anything. It is this: YOUR DEGREE OF SUCCESS IS DEPENDENT UPON YOUR PREVAILING MOOD OR FRAME OF MIND.

The pushing of any kind of business always commences in one's mind. The vision foreshadows the achievement. Every successful man today is living ahead of his business, and what he is accomplishing now was planned, thought over, and lived in for months and possibly years in advance.

When you stop planning improvements in your work, your business will begin to decline; you will continue to use your shop-worn line of selling talk while the live salesman next door is racking his brains for a new and better argument. Many a salesman is climbing to success over the backs of his competitors, and they, taking his dust as he passes, are blinded to opportunity and generally blame the house, or the product, or any old thing but themselves. The live man today refuses to use second-hand ideas. The man of initiative is the one who forgets the drag of the past and STARTS SOMETHING.

Another state of mind that has wrecked more salesmen than the armies of the world have killed men is FEAR OF THE CUSTOMER; fear of their ability to sell; fear that their cars are not equal to a competitor's; fear that the Big Man will kick them out of his office. Then you are a mere order taker. If you have a feeling of self-depreciation when you are calling upon a prospect, it's a mighty safe bet that the prospect won't regard you or your merchandise very highly unless the firm's advertising has been there first and made the sale before you arrived.

But why should you fear your prospective customer?

In all probability he will not hurt you—very much!

Yours is a plain business proposition: You are trying to sell him an article that will supply his needs. By making the sale you will help him while helping yourself. He can only buy—or refuse to buy. It's very doubtful if he ever did any serious bodily injury to a salesman who presented a business proposition to him in a business-like way. If you have confidence in your house and in the goods you are selling, and believe they are worth the price you are asking for them, your prospect is BOUND TO FEEL the same sort of confidence.

Once upon a time a prospective buyer entered the office of a motor car dealer and asked to be shown the latest model of the car he sold. He was welcomed by the manager, who quietly explained the merits of that model.

The man listened to the sales talk and asked many questions. Finally he said: "I came in to see this car out of curiosity. I'll have to confess that I had about made up my mind that I would buy a Blank Car. Your talk has not changed my decision entirely, and I'd like to see the other car before I buy."

Of course this manager, following the old methods, should have camped right on the job of telling this prospect how his own car was superior to the Blank. He didn't do anything of the kind. His prospect had expressed a desire to see the rival car before making a final decision—a right and privilege that should not be denied him.

"If you will step into my car," said the manager, "I'll have you taken to the Blank offices. The Blank car is a good one, and deserves your study. If, after comparing it point for point with our car, you decide that ours is the better, we shall be very happy to serve you."

This manager not only had the prospect carried to the rival showrooms, but instructed one of his salesman to accompany him and introduce him to the rival manager. The salesman introduced the man to the manager and told the latter that his visitor was in the market for a car and wished to have the Blank demonstrated. Then he withdrew. Later the prospect returned to the first dealer. "Your willingness to have me see the Blank car; your own admission that it was a good car to buy; your offer to take me to the rival showrooms and introduce me to the manager astonished me," said the buyer. "But I knew that you could not do as you did unless you had absolute confidence in your own car.

"You evidently had no FEAR of competition.

"Your own belief made me believe. I want YOUR car."

Right here, brother salesman, you have the bed-rock upon which the whole science of salesmanship is built—Conviction based on Confidence!

This is a true story, and it is a mighty sure proof that if you are confident, determined, pushing, hopeful, and, above all, your business is based on the RIGHT STATE OF MIND, your customers will FEEL that spirit and your success will grow accordingly.

Enthusiasm

Napoleon Hill

When your own mind is vibrating at a high rate, because it has been stimulated with enthusiasm, that vibration registers in the minds of all within its radius, and especially in the minds of those with whom you come in close contact. When a public speaker "senses" the feeling that his audience is "en rapport" with him he merely recognizes the fact that his own enthusiasm has influenced the minds of his listeners until their minds are vibrating in harmony with his own.

When the salesman "senses" the fact that the "psychological" moment for closing a sale has arrived, he merely feels the effect of his own enthusiasm as it influences the mind of his prospective buyer and places that mind *"en rapport"* (in harmony) with his own.

Source: *The Law of Success*. The Ralston University Press, 1928, Vol. IV, p. 91.